A HANDBOOK OF CANADIAN
LITERATURE

A

HANDBOOK

OF

CANADIAN

LITERATURE

by

V. B. RHODENIZER

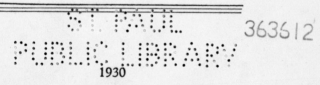
1930

GRAPHIC PUBLISHERS LIMITED

OTTAWA CANADA

Copyright *1930*
by
Graphic Publishers Limited

PRODUCED ENTIRELY IN CANADA
BY GRAPHIC PUBLISHERS PRESS,
AT OTTAWA, CANADA.

PREFATORY NOTE

This HANDBOOK differs from other Handbooks of Canadian literature in that it attempts three things not found elsewhere in combination,—a fresh and significant synthesis of biographical and historical details, a simple and practical guide to the appreciation of literary art, and an independent and judicial critical evaluation of the work of the authors discussed.

CONTENTS

PREFATORY NOTE 5
1. INTRODUCTION 11
2. PURITAN LITERATURE 18
3. LOYALIST LITERATURE 26
4. SCOTTISH LITERATURE 33
5. JOSEPH HOWE 40
6. THOMAS CHANDLER HALIBURTON 47
7. TRAVEL, EXPLORATION, AND MEMOIRS 55
8. HISTORY AND BIOGRAPHY 63
9. RISE OF THE CANADIAN HISTORICAL NOVEL...... 71
10. WILLIAM KIRBY 79
11. SIR GILBERT PARKER 87
12. OTHER NOVELISTS, HISTORICAL AND REGIONAL...... 95
13. SOME RECENT NOVELISTS 103
14. NATURE WRITERS I —
       WRITERS OF ANIMAL STORIES 111
15. NATURE WRITERS II —
       LOCAL COLOURISTS 119
16. CANADIAN ESSAYISTS 127
17. CANADIAN HUMORISTS 135
18. THE CANADIAN SHORT STORY 144
19. CANADIAN DRAMA 152
20. EARLY POETS 160

CONTENTS — *Continued*

21. CHARLES G. D. ROBERTS 170
22. BLISS CARMAN 178
23. WILLIAM WILFRED CAMPBELL 185
24. EMILY PAULINE JOHNSON 193
25. ARCHIBALD LAMPMAN 201
26. FREDERICK GEORGE SCOTT 208
27. DUNCAN CAMPBELL SCOTT 216
28. OTHER CANADIAN POETS TO SERVICE 224
29. CANADIAN POETS SINCE SERVICE 232
30. WILLIAM HENRY DRUMMOND 243
31. FRENCH-CANADIAN LITERATURE 251
32. CONCLUSION 261
SYLLABUS OF CANADIAN LITERATURE 268
INDEX 276

A HANDBOOK OF CANADIAN LITERATURE

Chapter i

INTRODUCTION

Who is a Canadian author? Canada, as she has developed from a colony to a nation, and acquired the measure of material prosperity essential to artistic creation, has had writers of several classes, according to the extent of their association with the country. As far as English-speaking Canada is concerned, there have been those who have had only an incidental and temporary residence in Canada; those who came to Canada in maturity and retained practically unmodified an Old-World point of view; those who, though foreign born, came to Canada in their tender years and grew up under Canadian influences; those who, though Canadian born and bred, sooner or later went to foreign lands to practise the profession of letters; those who, born and bred Canadian, have loyally and unselfishly practised the profession of writing under their native skies. What is true of the English-Canadian writers is true also of the French-Canadian, except that the latter have in a larger proportion remained in Canada.

Under the historic conditions it is obviously impossible to make a hard and fast definition of a Canadian author, or even to specify more than one or two characteristics that his work must have. If a writer's residence in Canada was only temporary and incidental, and his work shows no influence of Canadian nature or of Canadian life, he may reasonably be ruled out of the list of Canadian authors. But what of another author under identical conditions of residence whose work smacks of the soil or of the people or of both? Is Mrs. Jameson a Canadian author? She has given us "the best set of pictures available of Ontario as it was in 1836 and 1837." Again, what of the author born and bred in Canada who removes to some other country? Is he a Canadian author? No one would think of ruling out of the list of Canadian authors a native writer resident in Canada whose work makes no obvious specific reference to Canadian nature or Canadian life, because everybody knows that the mental store of images out of which he creates literature is derived from Canadian sources. This is almost equally true of the Canadian author resident abroad who has spent his most impressionable years under Canadian influences, and he should no more be ruled out of the list of Canadian authors than should Shelley and Browning be ruled out of the list of English poets because they lived part of their lives in Italy.

In this course we shall regard as legitimately entitled to consideration any work of literary quality that vitally touches the Canadian scene or the Canadian people in its subject matter, regardless of how incidental may have been the author's residential contact with the country; or that, though there may seem to be nothing distinctively Canadian in the material, has been written by authors born and bred in Canada, whether or not they have remained in the land of their birth.

The next matter of importance is how to study the body of material that, on the basis just set forth, may be regarded as Canadian literature. An excellent approach is made possible by a preliminary consideration of two points: first, De Quincey's distinction between the literature of knowledge and the literature of power; second, the manner in which the literature of power, as distinguished from the literature of knowledge, deals with the facts of life.

The literature of knowledge is written to inform, to convince, or to persuade. It is concerned with actual facts and people's opinions about, and actions in relation to, actual facts. It is assumed that it will not attain literary effectiveness by sacrificing truth to actual fact. This assumption, of course, is not always in accordance with actual fact. The literature of power, on the other hand, is not bound to the actual. It consists chiefly of imagined material, and it pictures scenes and events in order to give the reader a pleasurable emotional experience. On this basis of division, it is obvious that handbooks, most text-books, and in general newspaper and magazine material, belong to the literature of knowledge, and equally obvious that poetry and prose fiction belong to the literature of power. But the distinction is not always so easily made. There are border-line cases. From oratory, biography, history, memoirs, letters, and travel literature, the reader may derive not only information but also the type of pleasure that is associated with the literature of power. This suggests the pleasing possibility of passing by the way of an appreciation of the literature of knowledge to an appreciation of the literature of power.

We are now ready to consider the second point; the way in which the literature of power deals with the facts of life. This may be illustrated by a comparison with the way in which life is treated on the one hand by philosophy and on the other by science. Philosophy discusses life largely in abstract and general terms. It is concerned with ideas about life rather than with a concrete embodiment of those ideas in flesh and blood. Science, on the other hand, is largely concerned with concrete actual facts. Obviously, mankind needs an intermediary between the material of philosophy and that of science, between abstract ideas on the one hand and concrete individual facts on the other. It is the function of literature to embody the abstract ideas of philosophy and the concrete actual facts of science in a new creation of artistic truth. How is this done?

To produce literature, the abstract ideas about life (and every writer puts a philosophy into his work, will he, nill he) must be made concrete, not by using actual concrete facts, but by using imagined representative or typical facts. Take, for example, the general idea, "Fathers forgive wayward sons — and daughters." We admit its truth as a philosophical generalization about life, but how much are we moved by it? Science, on the other hand, might make a collection of cases

[14]

of actual fathers and wayward sons — or daughters — and find that in some individual cases the father does not forgive his wayward child. Whether he does or not, these actual cases might not be any more interesting than are some statistics on other matters. Now, let literature perform its function and make both philosophy and science live. Let the abstract idea be made concrete, not by taking into account all the actual facts of life as compiled by a scientific observation, but by taking typical or representative facts, and what is the result? We have the matchless story of the prodigal son, which is more essentially true to human nature than would be the actual story of a father who did not forgive. (All of this without taking into consideration the rich literary value of the symbolic meaning of the parable).

Let us take another example. We all admit the truth of the philosophical principle that slavery is grossly unjust, and yet our interest in the subject, stated in this abstract way, may be of the slightest. Statistical evidence of actual cases of such injustice might have little more effect on us than has a statement of the general principle. But how about our reading of *Uncle Tom's Cabin,* produced by the method of literature? It moved us profoundly, even though the facts are not now regarded as being typical.

To come nearer home, we all agree that for the future welfare of Canada as a nation there must be goodwill between English and French Canadians. We may know of actual cases where such goodwill is or is not shown. Neither the general idea nor statistics of actual cases, how-

[15]

ever, will arouse intense interest in the subject. But if we read Jean McIlwraith's *The Little Admiral,* a piece of literature written for the purpose of creating in English-Canadian boys a proper attitude toward their French-Canadian brothers, we shall feel a vital interest in the matter, an interest that could not be aroused by an abstract statement of the idea of Canadian brotherhood or by any statistical collection of facts on the subject.

This discussion of the way in which the literature of power deals with the facts of life makes evident, not only that it affects our emotions a great deal more strongly than the literature of knowledge usually does, but also that the former contains a higher order of truth than does the latter. The actual truth of the literature of knowledge may not be so essentially true as the typical or representative truth of the literature of power. The content of the former may be only the raw material which the writer of the literature of power uses in the creation of a higher order of truth and beauty.

This does not mean that we should despise the literature of knowledge. Both it and the literature of power have their place in human life in general and in Canadian life in particular. We have previously seen that an appreciation of the literature of knowledge may be a favourable introduction to the literature of power. We now see in addition that, since the literature of knowledge may furnish the raw material for the literature of power, the former may help us

to estimate the genuineness of what purports to be literature of power, to separate the chaff from the wheat.

All of this suggests that in the study of Canadian literature it will be excellent policy to begin with the literature
of knowledge, in which the standards of truth and beauty
are more familiar to the general reader, and then to pass
with growing appreciation and power of discrimination to
the higher levels of literary truth and beauty. In the following discussions, this method, in combination with reasonable attention to chronological order, will be adopted so far
as is practicable. That is, writing that is the record of actual
experience, such as journals, memoirs, travels, biography, and
history will be considered before the higher forms of imaginative literature, such as poetry, drama, and narrative fiction.
This method will furnish all who follow the discussions with
an opportunity to discern the relation between Canadian life
and Canadian literature, to develop a discriminating appreciation of the forms of the Canadian literature, and to ascertain whether there is a Canadian national sentiment of which
Canadian men and women of letters are the voice.

CHAPTER 2

PURITAN LITERATURE

The student of Canadian literature who approaches the subject in an historical frame of mind, will naturally ask whether the American Indians had a literature. This inquiry will be dealt with when we consider our Indian woman of letters, Pauline Johnson. The next question would be, what of literature during the French Period? Because so few English-Canadians read French fluently, and because so little of the French material has been translated into English, Canadian literary material written in French must unfortunately receive scanty notice, and that it seems best to leave till the latter part of the course. The study of the English-Canadian material begins with the Puritan era (say till 1783) in Acadia, or "Nova Scotia" (practically the Maritime Provinces, since Prince Edward Island became a separate province only in 1773, New Brunswick in 1784).

Why should there be a Puritan era in Nova Scotia? Of the people of New England, the stronghold of Puritanism, several classes, including traders, fishermen, and the younger sons of the colonial aristocracy, found it to their material advantage to carry on enterprises in Nova Scotia. Their development of the country, however, was at first intermittent because they hesitated to settle permanently in a country where the number of French-Catholic communities was rapidly increasing. The expulsion of the Acadians in 1755 not only removed this difficulty but also made possible a change from military control, naturally repugnant to the New Englanders, to civil government. Civil and religious liberty having been assured, when the Acadian lands were opened for settlement in 1760, there followed a considerable influx of reputable families, highly desirable as citizens, from different New England states, who established themselves in the villages formerly occupied by the Acadians. The Peace of Paris in 1763 increased the migration from the older colonies to Nova Scotia. During the years that followed, the number of settlers from New England increased to such an extent that, because of tradition and nearness to their old home, they made Nova Scotia a mere appendage of New England, even to the extent of transplanting characteristic institutions like the town-meeting.

The significance of this New England influence for literature lies, of course, in its effect upon the culture of the community. The settlers from New England were Congregationalists, with the result that their pastors were almost invariably Harvard men, as were also their schoolmasters. In Nova Scotia, as in New England, these Congregationalists had few interests outside their church. It is not surprising therefore, that their literary contribution is almost wholly

[19]

in the form of religious literature. Of this body of material the most noteworthy in Nova Scotia is the result not of conformity but of revolt.

Congregationalism had become practically an established form of religion. This condition of formality, in a community of instinctive dissenters, was bound to challenge dissent. In the older colonies the revolt began under Whitefield. The migration from New England to Nova Scotia took the revolt into the latter region, where, carried much farther and centering about one individual, "the Whitefield of the Province", it changed the ideals of the inhabitants to the extent that they, at first called the "New Lights", going one step farther than their leader seems to have done, broke away from Congregationalism and eventually became the Maritime Baptists.

The leader of the movement in Nova Scotia was Henry Alline (1748–84), whose religious experiences, as recorded in his own *Life and Journals,* challenge comparison at various points with those of John Bunyan and Saul of Tarsus. Alline was born at Newport, Rhode Island, the son of parents born and reared in Boston, who early began his secular and religious training. He writes of himself: "I was very early moved upon by the spirit of God, though I knew not then what ailed me." While yet young in years he developed a morbid fear of death and of God, Whom he conceived to be, as he understood the catechism, ill-natured and cruel. Such thoughts intensified his fear, and he suffered agony of spirit. To his other fears were added fear of the sea and of the Indians when his parents with their seven children, taking advantage of the opening up of the Acadian lands for settlement, moved to Falmouth, Nova Scotia, in 1760. In fact, fear of the Indians so revived and intensified his fear of death that he began to doubt God's care for men and was driven to the verge of suicide. He found no relief from his spiritual agony by living a moral life. When he joined in pursuits that to his Puritan ideas were sinful, thoughts of his lost condition so crowded his mind that he could derive no pleasure whatever from these activities. After nineteen years of agony of spirit, he was converted in 1775. His account of his conversion is one of the most striking records in the psychology of religious experience.

He writes: "One evening as I was taking a walk . . . . ., all of a sudden I thought I was surrounded with an uncommon light; it seemed like a blaze of fire; I thought it outshone the sun at noon day". He thought the judgment day had come. When he found that it had not, he resolved to make his salvation his only concern, but found no relief. Later, he says, "About midnight I waked out of sleep, I was surprised by a most alarming call as with a small still voice . . . . I thought I saw a small body of light as plain as possible before me". Another six weeks of spiritual agony, and then, realizing that he could do nothing of himself and submitting himself wholly to God, his whole being was pervaded by a rapturous sense of redeeming love. Immediately he felt the call to preach, and spent the greater part of the night in a spiritual ecstasy.

Believing that his attempts to obtain more education were thwarted by Providence, he began preaching in his home town in 1776. He soon became an evangelist, and during the period of the American Revolution conducted revivals with great zeal at many places in the Maritime Provinces. His comment on some of the places he visited is very illuminating as to his ideas and ideals. He found Halifax a "land of darkness." Later, he says of that city, "the people in general are almost as dark and as vile as in Sodom." Other places in Nova Scotia were almost equally "dark". Prince Edward Island had only three Christians (Alline spent comparatively little time in New Brunswick). "O the stupidity, blindness and miserable condition the world is in!" Anxious to preach in his native New England, Alline went there in 1783, in spite of the fact that his zealous labours had broken his health. After some preaching in Maine, he was forced to desist, and died at Northampton, New Hampshire. His headstone bears the inscription, "Apostle of Nova Scotia".

Alline's writings, prose and verse, are confined to the expression of his religious emotions and activities. His religious experience can be understood only in its relation to Congregationalism. While New England Congregationalism was becoming less and less enthusiastic from generation to generation, the more conservative of its adherents, to which group the Allines evidently belonged, kept close to the Calvinistic system of theology. Henry Alline's spiritual agony seems to have been the result in an ardently emotional nature of a conflict between an earnest desire implicitly to accept as authoritative a system of belief, and an unconscious intellectual rejection of some elements of that system. Once he became conscious of his intellectual difficulties with Calvinistic theology as well as of his own spiritual attitude, his religious rapture was as intense as his previous spiritual agony had been, hence the zeal with which he worked. His intense nature imparted to both his prose and verse a lyric quality, whether he is writing of spiritual agony or ecstasy.

The question naturally rises, Can the writings of a person of so highly individual a temperament be representative? The success that attended his evangelism indicates that his experiences were more or less typical, according to the intellectual and emotional nature of each, of the Puritan Congregationalists who became the Maritime Baptists. Or, as Baker puts it, "Alline's work, surpassing in human interest that of all his contemporaries, is the most vital evidence of the theological revolt that tended to unify, and also to isolate, the Puritan inhabitants of Nova Scotia." The Puritan contribution to Canadian literature was episodic. Their claim to a permanent contribution to Canadian culture depends upon the achievement of the educational institution which, inspired by the zeal to be expected from the followers of Alline, they founded—Acadia University.

The lyric heights to which Alline could attain in prose are exemplified by the following extract from the account of his conversion: "Attracted by the love and beauty I saw in his divine perfections, my whole soul was inexpressibly ravished with the blessed Redeemer; not with what I expected to enjoy after death or in heaven, but with what I now enjoyed in my soul: for my whole soul seemed filled with the divine being. My whole soul . . . . was now filled with immortal love, soaring on the wings of faith, freed from the chains of death and darkness, and crying out, my Lord and my God; thou art my rock and my fortress, my shield and my high tower, my life, my joy, my present and my everlasting portion."

In hymn XCIX of Book V, his "universal song", after calling on earth, mountains, ocean, rocks, trees, flowers, beasts, and birds to praise the great Creator, he continues:

> "Ye sparkling globes that dress the night,
> And spread your orbit spheres so true,
> While ye reflect a glimpse of light
> Roll round and speak His praises, too.
>
> And O ye crowds of Adam's race,
> Awake and bid your sloth adieu;
> Crowd in the courts of boundless grace,
> And sing Jehovah's praises, too."

The concluding stanzas maintain the lyric rapture of the beginning.

These quotations are sufficient to show that, though Alline's literary ability was confined to lyric utterance and to religious emotion as the material for lyric utterance, he achieved in that limited field an ecstasy of expression seldom equalled and perhaps never surpassed.

CHAPTER 3

LOYALIST LITERATURE

Puritanism, however much it may have affected Canadian religious, social, and civic institutions positively, and artistic production negatively, was little more than an incident in the development of Canadian literature. Before the inciting impulse of that incident had died out, the success of the American Revolution had driven large numbers of "Tories", or United Empire Loyalists, into Canada from the close of the Revolutionary War to the War of 1812. During this period English-Canadian literature had its real beginnings in Nova Scotia.

That these beginnings were in Nova Scotia rather than elsewhere in Canada, is explained by the fact that the refugees who settled in Nova Scotia represented "the highest traditions of American culture" whereas those who went to other parts of Canada were, with few exceptions, "from the humbler ranks of society." The Maritime Provinces received two hundred graduates of Harvard College and graduates of other colleges in similar proportion. Among this large accession of desirable citizens were outstanding repre-

[26]

sentatives of those who in the older colonies had been the "aristocracy of culture, of dignified professions and callings, of official rank and hereditary wealth."

These people brought with them literary ideals. As intellectual leaders some of them had taken part in the literary controversy that preceded the actual war for independence. The "Tories" regarded the idea of revolution as a thoroughly plebeian thing, and therefore as a fit subject for ridicule. This favoured the development of the satirical method in both prose and verse, and as the American colonies were still dominated by the influence of Dryden, Pope, and Churchill, the Loyalists brought into Canada the tradition of satire, and of the heroic couplet as a model medium for its expression in verse. At first they found little opportunity to make use of their literary traditions.

It must not be supposed that people of such social and cultured eminence as the Loyalists gladly exchanged the land in which they were so well established for the comparatively unsettled regions of Canada in which they were offered homes. "Most of them were compelled by official or unofficial persecution to leave the Old Colonies; and they looked forward persistently to the time when they could return." Jacob Bailey (1731–1808), whose *Journal* is one of the important records of Loyalist experience, writes: "When American Independence was announced to me, I was sitting in my study and employed in reading; but the instant this disagreeable sound struck my ears I continued motionless, frozen with horror, for the space of ten minutes . . . .

During the night I enjoyed but little repose. Interrupted slumbers, distressing dreams, and visions of terror were my constant attendants till the morning opened with a sullen and malignant light to renew a train of melancholy reflections." Again he writes: "The thoughts of being driven from our country, our much loved home, and all those endearing connections we had been forming so many years, and, if we escaped the angry vengeance of the ocean, the expectation of landing on a strange and unknown shore depressed our spirits beyond measure." Bailey's later records show that the anticipation did not exceed the first cruel reality, the suffering from hunger, cold, and disease.

The writings of the Loyalists are full of the homesickness of a people who regard themselves as exiles in an inhospitable climate. They are also full of a threefold despair: despair at the past because they had been defeated in what they regarded as a righteous cause; despair at the present because they were dissatisfied with each other, with the treatment they received from the British administration, and, in many cases, with the ideals of the Puritan settlers; despair at the future because the Proscriptive Acts passed by the revolted colonies destroyed all hope of return to the land of their birth, and they had yet no vision of happy homes in the land of their forced adoption.

The notes of home-sickness and of despair, dominating as they do Loyalist prose, find their fullest expression in verse. We may take the work of Joseph Stansbury (1740-1809) as an example, even though he was not a typical

[28]

Loyalist in the respect that he did not remain permanently in Canada. He had emigrated from England to Philadelphia, whence he was banished for singing the British National Anthem in his own house in 1776, and fled to New York. On settling in New Jersey after peace was concluded, he was imprisoned. Paroled on the condition of leaving the State within nine days, he came to Shelburne, Nova Scotia, one of the important Loyalist settlements, where he remained for two years. His Loyalist stand brought him ten years of persecution after his return to the United States.

Before the Revolution he had shown considerable skill in versification. During his two years in Nova Scotia he wrote his "To Cordelia", among the best verse of its time, and historically significant because it expresses, with simplicity and a measure of grace, characteristic early moods of the Loyalists in British North America.

A writer of verse who struck the chords of homesickness and of despair and who was also a typical Loyalist, in respect of permanent residence and otherwise, is the Jacob Bailey to whose prose writing reference has already been made, and whose "A Farewell", composed on the occasion of his expulsion from his New England home with its famous garden, contains some very fine passages of verse.

More important from a literary point of view than Stansbury or Bailey is Jonathan Odell (1737–1818). Descended from William Odell, one of the founders of Massachusetts, he was born at Newark, New Jersey. He was educated at the College of New Jersey, now Princeton University, of

[29]

which his maternal grandfather, Jonathan Dickinson, was the first president. After acting as surgeon in the British army in the West Indies, he went to England to take holy orders, and was made a priest in 1767. He became rector of St. Mary's Parish, Burlington, New Jersey. Though he was esteemed by his parishioners, though he was devoted to his religious duties, and though he consistently advocated the claims of the dissatisfied colonies, he was driven from his parish in 1777 because he opposed armed force. Hunted from place to place, he reached New York, where he became a Loyalist chaplain and satirist. At the close of the war, after a few months in England, he settled in New Brunswick and became an influential citizen. He and his family held public offices of distinction in his adopted province, at the capital of which he died.

At the beginning of the Revolution he was already an able writer of prose and verse, and he used his pen on the Loyalist side throughout the war. He was thus well qualified to bring into Canada the tradition of the English satirists, Dryden, Pope, and Churchill, to whom, as we have seen, cultured America looked for literary models. Though Odell was a poet of some range and taste outside the field of satire, he is of interest in the history of Canadian literature chiefly because he brought into Canada the tradition of Tory political satire and the heroic couplet, both of which influenced succeeding literary generations, and the former of which attained its last and greatest expression in the works of Haliburton.

The verse of Odell suggests further that after a period of home-sickness and despair the Loyalists began to feel at home in Canada. In time the expression of a proper hatred of United States and of a proper love of England became merely a matter of conventional good form, so that to the detrimental effect on literature of the almost exclusive use of eighteenth-century models was added the baneful influence of insincerity, a fault of which one feels Bailey and Odell were not guilty.

Other records of Loyalist experience in Canada are the collections of letters, the diaries and journals, both military and civil, and the attempts at history that belong to the period. In general, they belong to the literature of knowledge, with only here and there, as in the case of some parts of Bailey's *Journal,* passages that have some of the qualities characteristic of the literature of power.

However adverse the conditions in which the Loyalists found themselves in their new home, they strove to maintain their educational standards. The influence of Loyalist schoolmasters in the establishment of schools is hard to estimate. To the influence of the Loyalists, among them Jonathan Odell, is due wholly the founding of the University of King's College, and partly the establishment of Pictou Academy, both of which have exercised an incalculable influence on Canadian culture.

Further evidence of the efforts of the Loyalists to maintain their standards of culture is found in the pages of the loyalist reviews. The *Nova Scotia Magazine* (1789-91),

[31]

for example, had a twofold literary purpose: "to preserve and diffuse a taste for British literature"; to encourage "young writers among the rising generation to try their strength." To teach appreciation and to encourage creation is all that any institution can do for literature. The pages of the *Magazine* show, however, that the writers were not yet ready to be original. The contributions show that the authors still followed the literary models that they brought with them from their former home. The *Quebec Magazine* (1792–4), a monthly written in both French and English, the writers of which attempted to adapt their material to the needs of British North America, was equally short-lived.

That the Loyalists did not achieve more highly in literature is due at least in part to the conditions under which they lived. Perhaps none of them had the outlook on life, the power of imagination, and the skill in expression that are essential to the production of great literature. On the other hand, the arts cannot flourish while a people has to devote all of its energies to obtain the bare necessities of existence. Establishing themselves in a new land was necessarily a slow process for the Loyalists, and before this had been accomplished the War of 1812 precipitated new difficulties.

CHAPTER 4

SCOTTISH LITERATURE

The first large immigration of Scots into Canada took place three years before the outbreak of the American Revolution, and so antedates the coming of the Loyalists. The influence of these Scottish settlers, however, can best be sketched against the background of the Puritan and Loyalist immigrations. The few Puritan Congregationalists who did not become Baptists had joined the Presbyterian Church. Most of the Loyalists who did not belong to the Church of England did the same. When we consider that in 1773, driven from their native land by oppression, more than twenty-five thousand Highlanders settled in Cape Breton, in Prince Edward Island, and in various parts of the mainland of Canada, and that the communities thus formed were strengthened by other settlements, often of Lowlanders, so that centres like Pictou, Nova Scotia, and Glengarry, Ontario, were established, we are not surprised that before many decades the Established Church of Scotland had a strong following, especially in Nova Scotia.

[33]

Scottish immigrants of the type that settled in Pictou, brought with them two important ideals: that of "the supreme worth of the individual human spirit and its salvation" and that of sound education. So long as the University of King's College maintained the liberal policy of its founders — the only requirement was that the president should be a clergyman of the Church of England — there was no reason why Presbyterians should not be educated there without in any way compromising either of their ideals. In 1802, however, the reactionary forces were influential enough to induce the Imperial Government to pass an Act whereby only members of the Church of England could matriculate. No Scottish Presbyterian could now enter King's without feeling that he was compromising the first of the two ideals, the supremacy of the individual spirit, by becoming a member of a Church to whose tenets he did not hold. The result was that in 1819 the Presbyterians founded a school of their own, Pictou Academy, the intellectual influence of which on Canadian life has been very great and constitutes the greatest contribution of the Maritime Scots to Canadian culture.

In their new country both Highlanders and Lowlanders kept to themselves, and both, like the Loyalists, looked upon themselves as exiles in a foreign land. "As the Loyalists looked back to Boston, the Scotch looked back to Dundee", that is, with the same feeling of home-sickness. The literary significance of the Highlanders is chiefly historical in that some of their oral literature became attached to Canadian soil and assumed local significance. Unfortunately this folk-lore is dying out with the standardization that accompanies the conditions of modern life. The Lowlanders, apart from travel literature that will be considered elsewhere, contributed to Canadian letters nothing other than the sermons of their ministers. Like the Highlanders, however, they brought with them a body of oral literature, part of the English and Scottish popular balladry. Many of the Scottish settlers, struck by a wave of Puritanism, came to regard the singing of these ballads as sinful, with the result that decidedly more of them were preserved for posterity by Huguenot refugees who settled near the Scottish farmers than by the Scots themselves. Fortunately Nova Scotia has had in recent years an enthusiastic collector of this and similar material in W. Roy Mackenzie, whose *Ballads and Sea-Songs from Nova Scotia* is one of the most important contemporary collections of folk-lore.

The first sixteen numbers are "relics of the old English and Scottish popular ballads which came to Nova Scotia in the wistful memories of the Scottish settlers who migrated westward during the late years of the eighteenth and the early years of the nineteenth century." They are interesting versions and variants of the genuine English and Scottish popular ballads and show the changes that may result from oral transmission. They can be appreciated more fully by those who know some of the literary conventions of the popular ballads.

[35]

The typical ballad stanza consists of four lines of four and three feet, the first and third lines having four feet, the second and fourth, three. There may be two rhymes in a stanza or only one, the rhymes may be imperfect, and assonance may even take the place of rhyme. In telling a story, if there be more than one strong situation, the ballad is likely to dwell on one situation, leap abruptly from that to the next and dwell on it, and so on. Two kinds of repetition are of frequent occurrence, one in which there is repetition in direct or indirect discourse without in any way advancing the story, and the other in which such repetition does advance the story. The former is called parallel repetition, the latter incremental repetition. Some of the ballads, especially those that deal with a single situation, show a fine sense of the value of suspense in working up to a climax. Common subjects of popular ballads are: physical prowess, whether of individuals or of organized fighting forces; the comedies and tragedies of love between the sexes; love affairs between human beings and supernatural beings; supernatural visitations of human spirits.

Next to the material that the Scots brought with them we may consider anything they wrote in Canada in an imitative or reminiscent vein. There was a school of Burns in Canada, of which Alexander McLachlan (1818–96) was the most important member. Because of this rather doubtful distinction (judged by artistic standards) and because of the expression in his verse of the emotions that must have been somewhat typical of the Scottish settlers generally, he may appropriately be considered here, though his work falls in the latter half of the nineteenth century.

He was born of poor parents at Johnstone, Renfrewshire, Scotland. After a rather rudimentary education, he learned the tailor's trade at Glasgow, a fact to remember in connection with the then radical ideas that find expression in his verse. He came to Ontario, then Upper Canada, in 1840. Following several unsuccessful attempts at farming, he lived for twenty-five years on a one-acre lot at Erin, and then on his farm in the township of Amaranth until, shortly before his death, he went to live with his daughter at Orangeville. His closing years were made comfortable by the income from a sum of money raised for him by his friends, a noteworthy case in the annals of Canadian literature (and presumably his friends were Scottish, too).

Of special historic interest is McLachlan's projected pioneer epic, "The Emigrant", of which he completed the first part. The seven chapters of which it consists are entitled: Leaving Home, The Journey, The Arrival, Cutting the First Tree, The Log Cabin, The Indian Battle, Donald Ban. It was his intention to bring this history of a backwoods settlement, its scenes, incidents, and characters, up to the time of writing. Though this was never done, we can gather the history of the emigrant's emotion's from McLachlan's other poems.

One of the strongest lures to Canada was the possibility of owning a home. It is hard for a community unaccustomed to landlords to realize how this appealed to the Scottish settlers. No one has expressed this better than has McLachlan, unless it was the author of the ballad *Nova Scotia,* prefixed to Mackenzie's collection, of which the first stanza reads:—

"Let's away to new Scotland, where Plenty sits queen
    O'er as happy a country as ever was seen;
    And blesses her subjects, both little and great,
    With each a good house, and a pretty estate."

The reality did not always equal the expectation, and no Scot has voiced better than McLachlan the homesickness of the Scottish settlers. Another significant aspect of his poetry is that it shows the homesickness of the Scottish immigrant gradually giving place to a love of his adopted country. So complete is the transference of affection that a visit to his homeland fills him with disappointment and makes him glad to return to Canada as his true country.

We have said that McLachlan was the best of the imitators of Burns in Canada, and implied that this was not necessarily great praise. It is true that the Scottish lyrists in Canada were sincere, that they loved nature and humanity and hated political and religious hypocrisy and tyranny. But they lacked culture and the ability to criticize their own work. Though their intensity was sufficient to attain popularity with the uncritical masses of their day, a more cultured group of readers must judge them by their form as well as by their material. Their chief, McLachlan, in his humanitarian attitude toward common life and the lower animals, is morally and religiously more militant than Burns, but he is very inferior to Burns in range of lyric

[38]

expression. An eight-line stanza, often with double or internal rhymes, or both, and some false rhymes at that, is far too frequently his medium of expression, no matter what may be the lyric mood to which he gives utterance. In other words, he was far from being an artist in suiting his form to his subject matter. His place in Canadian literature, therefore, depends not on the quality of his art but upon the historical importance of his record of the changes in emotional attitude by which a Scottish immigrant becomes a Canadian citizen.

CHAPTER 5

JOSEPH HOWE
(1804-73)

We have seen the Puritan and Loyalist immigrants
separated from their kinsmen in the United States, the
former by theological revolt and the latter by political schism.
But the ties of blood are strong, in spite of family quarrels,
and the dependence to a considerable extent of the settlers
on Yankee papers, Yankee schools, and Yankee churches had
gradually produced a kindlier feeling between the two
kindred peoples. The growth of this feeling was accelerated
by the attitude of the ruling classes in Canada.

The press, the Church, and even educational institutions
came to be controlled by a governing minority, into whose
hands power had drifted during the period in which the inhabitants were wholly concerned with the arduous task of
making for themselves homes in a new land. Since the Coun-
cils, alone having the ear of the Imperial Government, were
supported by that government, there developed an attitude of
hostility toward Great Britain.

[40]

The War of 1812, which, as we have already noticed in passing, retarded even more the slow progress of the Loyalists in establishing homes in Canada, stopped the process by which the new colonies were again becoming assimilated to the old and developed to some extent a sense of unity among the hitherto isolated French, Loyalist, and Scottish elements of the population by giving them a common purpose, — resistance of the invaders. But the war intensified the evil of control centralized in a minority by putting more power in the hands of the ruling groups and by reducing the number of those who might have acted as leaders in the fight for the freedom of the press and for democratic principles in religion, education, and government. Obviously the first step was to free the press from the control of officialdom in order that the doings of officialdom might receive the scrutiny of the people.

It is difficult for people of the present day to realize the extent to which the newspapers were throttled. The Loyalists strove, among other things, to keep journalism alive. The leading newspapers of Philadelphia had been transferred bodily to Nova Scotia. But of the seven weeklies of some importance published in Canadian territory in 1812, Baker writes: "Any signs of editorial independence were ruthlessly suppressed, and one editor at least suffered imprisonment for his temerity in criticizing an unpopular measure. Nevertheless, in spite of this unreasoning censorship, several papers continued the Revolutionary temper. It is curious to notice how ridicule and burlesque were thus engrafted on the journalism of British North America." What was needed was a leader big enough to continue the "Revolutionary temper" and to employ the method of satirical journalism with sufficient power to liberate the press. Nova Scotia was fortunate enough to find that leader in Joseph Howe.

Four Howe brothers from Southern England had settled in New England early in the seventeenth century. Of thousands of descendants from these, at the time of the Revolution, only John Howe adhered to the side of England. He removed to Halifax, bringing with him the press of the *News-Letter,* the first newspaper printed in New England. In Halifax the *News-Letter* was amalgamated with the *Gazette,* and in Halifax, Joseph, the son of John Howe's second marriage, was born.

Joseph's formal education was rather meagre. In the summer he attended the school conducted by the famous Loyalist schoolmaster Bromley. At the age of thirteen, even summer attendance at school came to an end, and he entered his father's printing office. Joseph's slight formal education was supplemented by an informal education of great value. He spent as much time as he could in outdoor life, in conversation with his father, and in the reading of good books. This informal education resulted in a robust physique, a well-stored mind, and literary tastes and ambitions.

Probably because of the favourable notice taken of his poem *Melville Island,* he purchased the *Weekly Chronicle* in partnership in 1827, that is, at the age of twenty-three. Conducting this paper, as the *Acadian,* served to complete his training for the great task of his career, namely, conducting the *Novascotian,* which he purchased in 1828 and kept till 1841. Seven years of incessant labour on his part made it the leading newspaper of British North America in both political and literary influence.

In 1835 occurred an event of primary historical importance. Nova Scotia, like the other colonies, had long suffered at the hands of its governing bodies. At this time Howe published a letter signed "The People" accusing the magistrates of Halifax of misappropriation of public funds. Placed on trial for libel, Howe pleaded his own cause in a speech that lasted nearly six hours. Anyone who reads this speech will not be surprised at Howe's subsequent success as an orator or at the fact that he won his case, thereby winning for journalism in British North America its Magna Charta.

The next year, elected as member of the Assembly, Howe began his political career. His ideas on religious and educational matters show the same statesmanlike liberalism that he had exemplified in his attitude toward the press and that he was later to exemplify in his fight for representative government. Some of his ideas on religious and educational matters the people of his time were ready to put into effect. Others, such as the establishment of a central university instead of a number of denominational colleges, they were not ready to consider.

Noble as was Howe's liberalism on subjects religious and educational, it seems insignificant in comparison with

[43]

the magnificent statesmanship that, after a struggle of twelve years, won responsible government for Nova Scotia, and thus eventually for Canada, in 1848. From 1850 on, the recognition of his worth was abundantly manifested. He received such Provincial appointments as delegate to England on behalf of the Intercolonial Railway (1850), Chief Commissioner of Railways (1854), Premier of Nova Scotia (1860), and such Imperial appointments as delegate to the United States in connection with the Foreign Enlistment Act (1855), Fishery Commissioner to the United States (1863), and, to crown all, Lieutenant-Governor of Nova Scotia (1873). His tenure of this high office was terminated within a few days by his sudden death.

The Howes having been in New England for several generations, John Howe was, up to the time of the Revolution, thoroughly American in thought and feeling. To his son Joseph he imparted in large measure his knowledge of colonial history and ideals. It is to be expected, therefore, that the son's writings, however much they are the expression of the marked individuality of Joseph Howe, should show the influence of the Loyalist tradition, which, so far as literature is concerned, was, as we have already discovered, adherence to eighteenth-century English models. Howe's poems do reflect this literary attitude of the American colonies. Some of them are written in heroic couplets and some of his descriptive and narrative material is reminiscent of Goldsmith in its love of family life and of home scenes. His descriptive and reflective sketches, based on his travels in Nova Scotia, on the Atlantic, and in England, are reminiscent of the eighteenth-century essay in England, either directly, or indirectly through the influence of similar work by the American essayist, Washington Irving. The papers of *The Club* (1828–32), of which Howe was one of the leaders, reflect the spirit of personal and political satire developed in the Loyalists during the controversial stage of the Revolution. This spirit finds expression frequently, and often with great effectiveness, in the letters and speeches which constitute Howe's greatest contribution to Canadian prose in general, and which stand unsurpassed both for quality and for quantity in the political literature of Canada.

The question naturally arises, in view of this imitative or reminiscent aspect of Howe's work, whether he is of any more than historic importance. Are his writings, like those of the Puritans, Loyalists, and early Scottish immigrants, merely historic episodes without positive effect on the development of Canadian literature? Though Howe's work unmistakably shows the Loyalist regard for eighteenth-century English models in verse and prose, he made a very original contribution to Canadian literature. His journalistic writings during the first eleven years of his ownership and editorship of the *Novascotian,* contain vivid pictures of Nova-Scotian scenes and pointed comment on men and affairs in Nova Scotia, in a style that, though not always on the same high level, marks the beginning of a new epoch in Canadian prose. In the same way, traces of literary influence in his

[45]

political writings pale into insignificance in the original epic grandeur of his intellect and imagination as expressed in his views on responsible government, on the organization of the Empire, and on the future of British North America.

His contribution to pure literature, as distinguished from that which has a practical purpose, is contained in one volume, *Poems and Essays*. It is worth noting, to show the versatility of Howe's genius, that this volume contains a creditable attempt at fiction, "The Locksmith of Philadelphia." The so-called "Essays" were all delivered originally as orations. They show Howe's intellectual alertness to the movements of his day, his wide reading of world history and literature, his skill in drawing illustrations from his reading and from his personal experience, and his adeptness in bringing his general thesis to bear directly upon his particular audience. His poems range in emotional appeal from humour to pathos; they pay fitting tributes to the value of the commonplace in nature and in life (which they could not do if they slavishly followed eighteenth-century English models) ; they contain pleasing allusions to the joys of domestic life; and they paint pleasing word-pictures of Nova-Scotian scenery. His love of his native province, which, because of historical circumstances, was the only local patriotism with which he could supplement his noble Imperial sentiment, is well shown in his poem *Acadia*. Howe's achievements in literature and in statesmanship make it impossible for Canadians, even Nova Scotians, to over-estimate his importance.

CHAPTER 6

THOMAS CHANDLER HALIBURTON
(1796–1865)

In our study of Joseph Howe we had occasion to refer to *The Club*, which began in 1828 and continued with interruptions till 1832, of which Howe was one of the leaders, and the members of which met regularly at his house to plan their papers. The spirit of these papers is that of personal and political satire, the spirit which the Loyalists brought with them into Canada, which was used to such good effect by Howe in his political work, and which was to find its supreme literary expression in Thomas Chandler Haliburton, the most famous member of *The Club*.

Thomas Chandler Haliburton was born at Windsor, Nova Scotia, until recently the seat of the University of King's College. Like Sir Walter Scott, he was descended from the Haliburtons of Mertoun and Newmains, and if family tradition be correct, the great-great-grandfather of each was the same Haliburton. Thomas's paternal great-grandfather Andrew, and grandfather William, the latter of whom moved to Nova Scotia when the Acadian lands were opened for settlement, each married into the Otis family, and Thomas's mother, Lucy Grant, was the daughter of one of Wolfe's officers, Major Alexander Grant. Thus born into a good social position in an environment in which both town and gown fostered "Tory" sentiment, Haliburton attended the Grammar School at Windsor and later, in 1815, graduated with honours from the University.

The next year he married Captain Lawrence Neville's daughter Louisa, who lived till 1840 and bore him seven children. Called to the bar in 1820, he practised law at Annapolis Royal, and in 1826, evidently on the strength of his ability as a pleader, was made representative of the County in the Nova Scotia House of Assembly. Two years later, when the death of his father left vacant the position of Chief Justice of the Court of Common Pleas, Haliburton received the appointment and lived quietly at Clifton, his Windsor estate. On the abolition of the Court of Common Pleas in 1841, Haliburton was appointed to the Supreme Court. In 1856 he resigned, moved to England, received an honorary D.C.L. from Oxford, refused a governorship, and married a cultured and affectionate English widow. In England he made literary friendships (one with Barham of "Ingoldsby Legends" fame) and achieved a reputation as a conversationalist. Elected through the influence of the Duke of Northumberland to the House of Commons in 1859 as member for Launceston, Haliburton ineffectively advocated the unpopular cause of imperialism.

[48]

By 1865 he found his health too much impaired to offer himself for re-election, and he died August 27th of that year.

Haliburton's work, taken as a whole, is the culminating expression of the spirit of political and personal satire brought into the Maritime Provinces by the Loyalists, notably by Jonathan Odell and his associates. Not all of his writing, however, is of equal literary value. His merits and defects may conveniently be considered by taking up his work according to the divisions made by Baker: first, the historical and political treatises; second, the *Slick* series; third, miscellaneous fiction that continues the methods of the *Slick* series; last, anthologies of American stories, of which he was the editor.

The material of the first group clearly belongs to the literature of knowledge. Haliburton had a practical purpose and pursued practical methods of writing. Haliburton, like Howe, believed firmly in Nova Scotia and never ceased to proclaim its advantages. In 1823 appeared an anonymous pamphlet entitled *A General Description of Nova Scotia,* a vindication of the soil, climate, and resources of Nova Scotia against persistent and uninformed disparagement. Chittick has shown that this pamphlet was written by Haliburton. In 1829 he published *An Historical and Statistical Account of Nova Scotia.* His political writings, which reflect his interest in the future of British North America in relation to the Empire, cannot be considered in detail. Of his historical and political writings in general as a manifestation of the spirit of political and personal satire, it may be said that they are neither good history nor good literature, for he was too biassed a "Tory" and Churchman to interpret his material fairly even when he had the facts (in some cases he could not get, or was too indolent to get, the facts), and the form in which he presented his material falls below the level of literary art. These pamphlets and treatises are important because they show the prevalence among Canadians of the belief in monarchical government and imperial connection and of the mood that satirized republican government as being essentially plebeian, the mood that prevails in Haliburton's greatest work, the *Slick* series.

Sam Slick so astonished the reading world that he was regarded as being more original than he really is. As a matter of fact, the nature of his adventures shows that he is a lineal descendant from the *picaro,* the rogue or rascal who in Europe gave the name to a whole school of literature, the picaresque novel, or the literature of roguery. The rogue or rascal in Haliburton's *Slick* series took the form of a New England pedlar of clocks because Haliburton had had actual experience in Nova Scotia with a pedlar of the kind and because a Yankee pedlar was a stock figure on the English stage. He spoke in dialect because two American writers had furnished Haliburton the precedent of dialect and because a taste for dialect had been fostered by the papers of *The Club.*

The other central character of the *Slick* series is a Squire who encounters Slick while both are travelling about the country. The literary precedent for the Squire's journeying is the travel literature of the time. The whole action of the series, therefore, is a fusion of travel literature, represented by the Squire, with the literature of roguery (also largely travel literature), represented by Sam Slick.

There still remains the question how Haliburton, the aristocrat by birth and breeding, could so successfully characterize Sam Slick, the vulgar pedlar. The Squire, obviously, represents the aristocratic Haliburton, but how account for Slick? The answer that has been given is that Haliburton himself was a strange mixture, a dual personality, one side of which was essentially patrician, the other essentially plebeian. In this view, Sam Slick is a concrete embodiment of the vulgar, plebeian aspect of Haliburton's personality.

This study of the literary origins of the *Slick* series is of more than passing significance. It shows the continuity of literary development. No matter how original a piece of work may seem to be, it always has some connection with literary tradition. Genius manifests itself not by inventing something entirely new in form or substance but by adapting old material or old forms or both to a new set of conditions, and there is enough of this adaptation in the series to warrant the application of the term genius to Haliburton.

The success of the *Slick* series depends upon its humour, resulting from irreverence, irrepressibility, and humorous exaggeration in details and in the narration of anecdotes and incidents; upon its fresh and original expression in malapropisms, comparisons, figures of speech, and aphorisms; above all, upon the skill in characterizing not only the Squire

[51]

2

and the Clockmaker, but scores of Haliburton's own beloved countrymen in their native environment. From the literary point of view it is also of interest to notice that Haliburton has here employed the methods of the literature of power to practical ends. In his political and historical writing he had a practical purpose, and his method was the exposition or narration of facts as he interpreted them. In the *Slick* series his practical purpose is twofold: the satirizing of his countrymen for their dependence upon government and their lack of faith in their native land; and the advocacy of monarchical government and Imperial connection. But instead of resorting to the use of actual facts, he adopts the method of fiction, that is, he employs representative or typical facts (of course often exaggerated for humorous or satiric purposes), thereby making a much more powerful presentation of his ideas. There is thus in the *Slick* series enough of the creative imagination to make it the supreme expression of the satiric tendency of the Loyalist tradition.

It must not be supposed that the three series of *The Clockmaker* constitute the whole of the *Slick* series. The appreciation of *The Clockmaker* was so widespread that Haliburton made Slick an *attaché* of the American Legation in London. His fictitious adventures in this official capacity are recorded in *The Attaché; or Sam Slick in England,* of which there were two series, in 1843 and 1844 respectively, each series containing two volumes. Although Haliburton did not know England as he knew Nova Scotia, the semblance of truth was great enough to make some reviewers believe that Sam Slick represented some person actually resident in London. The high comedy that results from the vulgarity of Sam Slick in contrast with the politeness of the society in which he moves in England, is further proof of the genius of Haliburton in discerning what makes good comic material. Nevertheless, the praise of *The Attaché* was not nearly so general as the praise of *The Clockmaker* had been. In the rest of the *Slick* series, *Sam Slick's Wise Saws and Modern Instances; or What he Said, Did, or Invented* (one edition of which bears the sub-title *Sam Slick in Search of a Wife*) and *Nature and Human Nature*, Haliburton wisely returns to Nova Scotia as his scene of action, thereby largely re-establishing his reputation.

The third division of Haliburton's work, miscellaneous fiction, advocates the same ideas that are set forth in the serious aspect of the *Slick* series, and follows the methods of that series except that the characters are different. The writings of this group, in spite of Haliburton's characteristic weaknesses — over-emphasis of detail, broad typification, and lack of constructive skill — are further evidence of his power in description and in characterization.

Haliburton's work as editor of two collections of American humorous sketches is the result of his regarding himself as the apostle of American humour. These anthologies had a vogue across the Atlantic and helped to bring about a better understanding between England and the United States. They suggest also the sense in which Haliburton is "the father of American humour": not in the sense that he invented something entirely new, but that he gathered up various strands and gave them a supreme expression in his own work and encouraged the appreciation of other American humorists.

With regard to his influence on other writers, in England Haliburton's Sam Slick and the Squire seem to have suggested Dickens's Sam Weller and Pickwick. In the United States, the humorists in general and "Artemus Ward" and "Mark Twain" in particular show strong indebtedness to the *Slick* series. In Canada, the humorous parts of De Mille's travel fiction owe much, either directly, or indirectly through "Mark Twain", to the work of Haliburton.

CHAPTER 7

TRAVEL, EXPLORATION, AND MEMOIRS

We have seen the early settlers, Puritan, Loyalist, and Scottish, either too busy wresting homes for themselves from the primeval forest to record their experiences, or, when they found time to record them, doing it in a style too imitative or too formless to have permanent literary value, whatever the historical importance of their records may be. We have seen two sons of established Loyalist families making a permanent contribution to Canadian literature. We now turn to a group the mere stories of whose lives, regardless of anything they wrote, have an almost epic interest because they display two types of heroism: that of the men who travelled and explored, and that of the women who left the culture of an old civilization to make homes for their children in the forests of a new country.

Of the travellers and explorers, one of the most famous is Alexander Henry (1739–1824). He was born in New Jersey, of respectable middle-class parents said to have come from Western England, who evidently gave him a good English education. In his twenty-first year, Wolfe's victory at Quebec having awakened hopes of gain in the fur trade after the conquest, Henry joined Amherst's army and had his baptism of fire at Fort Levis in 1760. By August of the next year he was ready to set out from Montreal on the travels and adventures in "Canada and the Indian Territories" that kept him away from Montreal until October, 1776. The ensuing winter he spent in England and France. He returned in the spring of 1777, revisited the Indian country, and again crossed the Atlantic in the fall of the same year. On his return in 1781 from a third visit to Great Britain, he resided in Montreal. As a merchant and fur trader until 1796, and as a merchant only after that date, his integrity was such that in 1812 he was made King's Auctioneer, an appointment that he held until his death.

Henry's one work of literary merit, *Travels and Adventures in Canada and the Indian Territories between the Years 1760 and 1776*, of course belongs to the literature of travel and exploration. Historically it is important as the chief monument of the fur trade. Its errors in such matters of detail as distance and chronology detract nothing from the undeniable charm of its vividly accurate pictorial and atmospheric description and of its natural, direct, Defoe-like method of narration. These qualities make it one of the few pieces, if not the only piece, of writing of its kind in Canadian literature to rise to the realm of art. Among passages that illustrate Henry's literary qualities may be mentioned his account of the Pipe of Peace and that of the capture of Michillimackinac.

Another famous traveller was Alexander Mackenzie (1763–1820). He was born at Stornaway, Island of Lewis, Scotland, and seems to have received a fair education before he came to Canada at the age of sixteen in 1779. After five years of employment with John Gregory, Montreal merchant, he became, at the instance of his employer, a partner in a new fur-trading company. While at his first post, Grand Portage, he was placed in charge of the English River (Churchill) outfit. On the amalgamation of his company with the North West Company in 1787, he was sent to Fort Chipewyan, on Lake Athabaska, later his point of departure on and arrival from his famous journeys. In the course of the first, from June to September, 1789, he discovered the river that now bears his name and followed it to the Arctic Sea. Having spent the winter of 1791-2 in England in the acquirement of mathematical knowledge and technical equipment, he made his journey by land to the Pacific and back between the autumn of 1792 and that of 1793. After one more winter at Fort Churchill, Mackenzie returned to Grand Portage. He remained with his company until, on the expiration of his agreement, he went to England in 1799. In 1802 he received knighthood, projected unsuccessful colonization schemes, and returned to Canada. Here he participated for two years in the rivalry of the fur-trade companies, and was elected to parliament. He retired to Scotland in 1808. Four or five years later, by his marriage with a rich namesake, he acquired an estate in Rosshire. Here he resided until, taken suddenly ill while travelling, he died, away from home.

To the literature of travel and exploration belongs Mackenzie's *Voyages from Montreal* . . . . , a record of great historical significance not only because it contains important information about the Northwest but also because it stimulated explorers like Fraser and Thompson and settlers like Lord Selkirk. The author himself calls attention to the fact that he is not an artist in description and narration, but justifiably claims "the approbation due to simplicity and truth." These stylistic qualities combined with the intrinsic interest of the material will enable the modern reader to understand Napoleon's appreciation of the *Voyages,* especially if the reader is able to know at first hand Mackenzie's accounts of the Slave Indians, of amateur surgery, of the position of women, of an accident in the rapids, of an attack, and of an Indian village.

Of other literature of travel and exploration, some idea may be derived from the historical handbooks or the anthologies. The points to be considered in any literature of the kind are: Is it valuable as literature of knowledge? To what extent does it manifest the qualities of the literature of power? These qualities are present in a marked degree in the memoirs of several cultured women who, in a very restricted sphere as compared with that of the travellers and explorers, wrote of what they experienced in Canada.

Most readers will be surprised to meet here a woman whom they have long known as a Shakespearean critic, especially for her studies of Shakespeare's women. Mrs. Anna Brownell (Murphy) Jameson (1794-1860) was born at Dublin, Ireland. The daughter of a miniature painter, she became an artist and art critic of note. That her first literary work was a book of Italian travels is significant from the point of view of her contribution to Canadian literature, for it is through her *Winter Studies and Summer Rambles,* written during a visit to Canada in 1836–7, that she is entitled to consideration in any comprehensive study of Canadian literature.

Her keen power of observation, her artistic sensibility, her deep sympathy, her penetrating insight into character, and her special skill in expressing the results of all of these in vivid descriptive sketches, both pictorial and atmospheric, and in character studies, make this Canadian material "the best set of pictures available of Ontario as it was in 1836 and 1837." The *Studies and Rambles* should be read entire, with particular attention to her descriptions of Niagara Rapids, of Niagara in winter, of forest scenery, of Woodstock church, and of Indian customs, and to her analysis of characters and social customs.

By way of introducing the remaining two women, an account of the Strickland family of which they were members will be of interest. Thomas Strickland, an eccentric but brilliant Englishman, lived first at the Laurels, then at Stowe House, and finally at Reydon Hall, Suffolk. Of nine children born to him by his second wife, six born between the years 1794 and 1809, both inclusive, distinguished themselves more or less by their literary talent. When the father died in 1818, leaving the family in straitened circumstances, the two elder sisters, Elizabeth and Agnes, whose education had been completely in the hands of their father and who had already begun to write, found it necessary to use their pens as a part of their means of livelihood. Agnes wrote some verses and then, with her sister, some books for children. She is best known for her *Lives of the Queens of England,* the original edition of which included twelve volumes, and in the writing of which her sister Elizabeth collaborated. Agnes later edited the letters of Mary Queen of Scots, and wrote more biographies and fiction. She also edited for her brother Samuel his *Twenty-Seven Years in Canada,* recording his experiences subsequent to his coming to Canada in 1825, where he became connected with the Canada Company, and obtained the commission of major in the militia.

From the point of view of Canadian literature, the most important member of this talented family was Susanna (1803–85). She too was taught by her father and essayed fiction for the young. She married Lieutenant J. W. D. Moodie in 1831, and the next year came with him to Canada. They bought a farm near Port Hope, but soon disposed of it to settle on four hundred acres, in the unbroken bush ten miles north of Peterborough, granted to Lieutenant Moodie as a retired English officer. Here Mrs. Moodie and the family were left while Lieutenant Moodie, who became a captain, helped to suppress the rebellion of 1837. In 1839

Moodie was appointed Sheriff of Hastings County, and the family moved to Belleville.

Both Mrs. Moodie's prose and her verse show that she was influenced by the attitude of the English romanticists toward nature and the common life. At first, it is true, the contrast between the new and the old is to her a source of pain, but her writings reveal the gradual growth of a sympathetic attitude toward Canadian scenes and life. This attitude, combined with skill in description and in characterization of pioneer types, produced not only the best transcript we have of the conditions under which the early English settlers lived, but also a clear record of the emotional change that transformed cultured English men and women, homesick for their mother land, into loyal citizens with a strong sense of nationality and unbounded faith in the future of Canada. In *Roughing It in the Bush,* her best work, there are vivid descriptions of the journey up the St. Lawrence, of the environment of their new home, and of various kinds of new neighbours, and vivid narratives of adventures with fire, storms, and wild beasts.

The life of Catharine Parr (Strickland) Traill (1802–99), an elder sister of Mrs. Moodie and wife of one of Moodie's lieutenants, is closely parallel both in England and in Canada with that of Mrs. Moodie. Traill, an Oxford man, by correspondence kept in touch with progress in England. Hence his wife, like Mrs. Moodie a leader in the new Canadian aesthetic movement, was also, like her, influenced by the English romanticists. Her love of nature led her to

[61]

study Canadian plant life so carefully that she received from both the British and the Canadian Government material recognition as a naturalist. Her literary work, though lacking in narrative skill, contains accurate description, as a reading of *Canadian Crusoes,* a story of lost children, clearly shows. Her sympathetic stories of animal life may be regarded as the first animal stories in Canadian literature, a type that became important enough to be the subject of a later chapter in this course.

CHAPTER 8

HISTORY, BIOGRAPHY, AND AUTOBIOGRAPHY

The Canadian literary material previously considered has been in all cases largely, and in many cases wholly, based on the actual experiences of the writers. Even such outstanding men as Howe and Haliburton are not exceptions. Howe's work is mostly a by-product of his life activities, and Haliburton drew freely on his own actual experience in building up his rambling fictions. The autobiographical note is strong in McLachlan's poetry, and Alline's prose and verse are the records of his individual religious experience. Diaries, journals, memoirs, and the literature of travel and exploration are in the main fragments of autobiography, and the transition from them to sustained autobiography is an easy one for the student of literature to make. Autobiographies are only a specialized class of biographies, and history may be regarded as the biography not of individuals but of nations. We shall first endeavour to discover what is essential to the successful writing of history, the biography of nations, and then consider biography and autobiography in the light of our findings.

Why is it that, of all the vast number of books on Canadian history, as indicated in the handbooks of Canadian literature, so very few are regarded as having high literary quality? Are the writers of these history books lacking in one or more of the qualities that a good historian should possess? What are these qualities?

In our study of the nature of literature, we considered the method of the literature of power in dealing with the facts of life in contrast on the one hand with the method of philosophy and on the other hand with the method of science. We saw that every maker of literature is a philosopher. Unlike the professional philosopher, however, he cannot present his philosophy in the form of abstract discussion but must embody it in a concrete representation of human experience. In his use of the concrete, the author resembles the scientist, but differs from him in that he may use the typical or representative concrete, whereas the scientist is tied to the actual. How does the historian compare with the typical maker of literature in these respects?

The historian has less freedom than most other writers in that, like the scientist, he is tied to the actual. He must be as careful as the scientist to make sure that he has the actual facts. From these actual facts he has to select, to build up his narrative, with as great care as the typical writer has to select from his representative facts, which may have been more easily acquired than the historian's actual facts.

Thus, on the scientific side the historian has a harder task than the typical maker of literature. He will be condemned for inaccuracy in detail or for lack of proportion in selecting his material.

The successful historian must also be philosopher enough to perceive, understand, and explain the basic qualities in men and in their environment that caused to unfold the panorama of events which he records. He will be condemned if, as more than one historian has done, he interprets events to support preconceived prejudices or theories instead of forming conclusions only after the most detached study of the events.

But being a great scientist and philosopher will not make a great historian without the power characteristic of the makers of literature, namely, the power of imagination, that is, the power of presenting vividly, through the medium of language, scenes and events of which history is so largely composed. The nature and importance of this power in the historian, and the principle on which historians should choose their facts, were never more clearly set forth than by Macaulay, and we can do no better here than to use his exact words:

"While our historians are practising all the arts of controversy, they miserably neglect the art of narration, the art of interesting the affections" (meaning the emotions) "and presenting pictures to the imagination. That a writer may produce these effects without violating truth is sufficiently proved by many excellent biographical works . . . . . That history would be more amusing if this etiquette were relaxed will, we suppose, be acknowledged. But would it be less dignified or less useful? What do we mean when we say that one past event is important and another insignificant? No past event has any intrinsic importance. The knowledge of it is valuable only as it leads us to form just calculations with respect to the future . . . . . A history in which every particular incident may be true may on the whole be false. The circumstances which have most influence on the happiness of mankind, the changes of manners and morals, the transition of communities from poverty to wealth, from knowledge to ignorance, from ferocity to humanity — these are, for the most part, noiseless revolutions. Their progress is rarely indicated by what historians are pleased to call important events. . . . The perfect historian is he in whose work the character and spirit of an age are exhibited in miniature. He relates no fact, he attributes no expression to his characters, which is not authenticated by sufficient testimony. But, by judicious selection, rejection, and arrangement, he gives to truth those attractions which have been usurped by fiction."

It is of interest to note in passing that Macaulay applies even to history the principle set forth in our discussion of the literature of power, namely, that truth to fact may not be essential truth. More significant for the present discussion is his emphasis on the importance, in historical writing, of imaginative power, that is, of the power of presenting vividly scenes and events. In the exercise of this power the

[66]

historian has a twofold difficulty: first, he is bound to the actual for his material; second, his experience of that actual of necessity is at best only secondhand.

An examination of the vast mass of Canadian historical writing would, probably, show that the reason so little of it is distinctive is not that the writers were deficient in scientific accuracy or in philosophical insight but that they lacked imaginative power. From the few praiseworthy histories by Canadian historians we have singled out Roberts's *History of Canada*. Is this any more scientifically accurate than any other Canadian history? Is it more philosophical? Do we not, in fact, feel that Roberts allows his personal feelings to enter too largely into his discussions of the American Revolution, the struggle for responsible government, and the Canadian and Northwest rebellions? The real point of superiority in Roberts's history as compared with most others is its imaginative power. Whether or not it has more of this than other Canadian histories that are approximately its peers, it is an easy one from which to illustrate the effectiveness of the imaginative quality in historical writing.

In describing the expulsion of the Acadians, for example, Roberts writes: "Down to the flat red shore rumbled and creaked the rude Acadian carts, heaped with household treasures; and beside the carts moved the weeping peasant women, their bewildered children clinging to their skirts." Vivid as the whole of this passage is, the crowning touch is

[67]

the use of the adjective "red" to describe the shore, as any person familiar with the scene will at once recognize.

Again, writing of Braddock's defeat, Roberts says: "At a signal from this apparition there shrilled the daunting war-cry of unseen savages; and out of the sunny leafage on either hand streamed a murderous storm of lead." Here the adjective 'sunny" vivifies the picture as the word "red" does in the preceding quotation.

In the account of the final fall of Louisburg Roberts combines powerful appeal to the emotions with vivid picture: "For months went on the toil of demolishing the mighty fortifications — blowing up casemates, filling in ditches, shattering the walls of stone with pick and crowbar — till Louisburg was no more. But the vast lines of the earth-works are still to be traced, covered with a mantle of green turf; and the bells of pasturing sheep tinkle softly over the tomb of the vanished fortress."

Or take this passage from the description of the Mira-michi fire: "All through the day of that memorable October 7th, the townsfolk had been weighed down by the sultry, poisoned air, and by a dread of coming woe. The cattle, warned by a like instinct, huddled together in frightened groups; and wild animals, tamed by fear, crept out of the woods to seek refuge in the clearings. About sundown came the first huge breaths of a burning wind, and through the sudden darkness could be seen the red flashings and creep-ings of the fire along the western sky. Soon the wind grew to a wild gale, and up from the horizon's edge the flames

[68]

leaped ominously. Then came an appalling roar, that bowed men's souls with terror; the sky rained hot cinders and flaming branches; and the heavens grew suddenly one sheet of flame." Here we have picture, atmosphere, and emotion combined in the most effective manner, and this is the work of the imagination. Be a historian never so good a scientist and philosopher, he will not be effective unless he has also imaginative power.

The same is true of the biographer. And his difficulty is exactly that of the historian: he is tied to the actual and he has to experience that actual largely at second-hand. May it not be that the scarcity of great biography in Canada, as of great historical literature, is due to the lack of imaginative power in the presentation of the material?

Autobiography, on the other hand, should be strongest in the respect in which history and biography are likely to be weakest. Any person who would write a story of his own life is likely to have in a high degree what is called the artistic temperament. He would observe accurately, respond to stimuli with more than average sensibility, and record his experiences in the most effective language. He would do the last not only because he was writing from first-hand experience but because a gift for apt phrasing is one of the outstanding characteristics of the artistic temperament. Of this temperament we can find perhaps no clearer illustrations than Michael Williams and F. P. Grove in the *High Romance* (1918) and the *Search for America* (1927) respectively. As long as they are recording their experiences

[69]

with imaginative power they carry us along with them and hold us spellbound. But what happens when they begin to philosophize about the experience? Even the mild amount of interpretation in Grove challenges at times our disagreement. And certainly many will refuse to agree with the thesis that Williams so persistently argues, the necessity of the universal adoption of the Roman Catholic form of Christianity. Autobiography, then, has a natural advantage over biography and history in imaginative power only, and more of this quality will improve Canadian biography and history.

Of many Canadian writers on historical subjects, one who has written a sufficient amount to be called a professional historian and whose work has imaginative power enough to entitle it to consideration as literature, is Lieutenant-Colonel William Charles Henry Wood (1864–........), retired Canadian army officer. He was born at Quebec and educated at Wellington College, England, and in Germany. His interests have been historical and military. Since 1904 he has published many volumes of historical material, a goodly number of which have been on Canadian subjects, particularly on aspects of French-Canadian history. His work is valuable not only for its literary quality but also for its stimulus to the development of national consciousness and of a sense of unity among Canadians, whether they speak English or French.

CHAPTER 9

RISE OF THE CANADIAN HISTORICAL NOVEL

From the preceding study we arrived at the conclusion that the cause of ineffectiveness in historical writing is most likely to be lack of imaginative power and that this lack may be partly due to the twofold difficulty under which the historian writes; namely, his being bound to the actual and his having to experience that actual largely if not wholly at second hand. To what extent the writer of historical fiction is released from the restrictions placed on the historian depends on the nearness of the fictionist to, or his remoteness from, the historical facts of which he makes use, and on whether he is a romanticist or a realist. Even the latter, however, would feel free to introduce fictitious characters and occurrences along with his historical people and events, and a romanticist would take even greater liberties. Whether or not historical fiction is romantic or realistic depends partly on popular taste, partly on the kind of medium through which the author may reach his readers, and partly on the temperament of the author and the nature

[71]

of his experience of life. In the case of Major John Richardson (1796–1852), the tendency was toward romanticism in all of these respects.

Whereas the Loyalists had brought to the Maritime Provinces the pseudo-classic tradition, the cultured British settlers in Ontario during the first half of the nineteenth century brought with them the ideals of romanticism. By the time that Richardson was a young man, romantic historical narrative had found expression in two adequate forms in the English tongue, — the metrical romance, as exemplified in the work of Scott and Byron, and the romantic historical novel, in which the most significant work, from the point of view of a study of Richardson, was that of Scott and Cooper. That Richardson was well aware of the advantage of using forms that had already been favourably received, is shown by the fact that he actually attempted the metrical romance in his *Tecumseh*. His shrewd observation, coupled with his artistic sense, must have told him that the form of the immediate future was not the metrical romance but the historical novel, because it was better adapted to popular taste and because it was a form better suited to his material. Moreover, in addition to the book form there was a serial market for romantic material, especially after the founding of the *Literary Garland* (1838–51), which favoured romanticism and the use of Canadian material.

A suitable form in which to gratify the popular taste for romanticism being thus available, Richardson most assuredly had the temperament to give his material romantic treatment. Although the use of a great deal of actual fact from first hand personal experience gives to his work a strong impression of truth to life, he did not hesitate to depart from fact to make a better story. On the grounds of art he justifies himself in the alteration of geographical fact in such matters as the distance between two places or the size of a river, or of historical facts in the way of introducing anachronisms or of putting events earlier or later than they occurred in the actual sequence.

Family tradition, environment, and personal experience all combined to make Richardson a romanticist. On both sides he was descended from people who had supported the lost cause of the Stuarts, and his name is associated with the French, Scottish, and Loyalist elements of Canadian history. He was born at Queenston, Ontario, in 1796, the year of Haliburton's birth. His father, Robert Richardson, a military surgeon, was a native of Annandale, Scotland. His mother was Madeleine Askin (originally Erskine), daughter of a Scottish Loyalist and wealthy merchant, John Askin, who married into an aristocratic French family. In 1801 Richardson's mother and her family went to live for nearly a year with her father at Detroit. Then the family settled at Amherstburg, where Richardson was reared and educated. His mother taught him to read and write French. Of his attitude to formal education he says of himself: "I had ever hated school with a most bitter hatred." In spite of this, because of his native brilliance he did well in subjects other than French. When war gave him an opportunity to get away from school, he gladly availed himself of it. In the ranks of the Forty-First Regiment from July 9, 1812, he engaged in active service until he was captured at Moraviantown in 1813. Released the next year, military life kept him moving until his settlement in London on half-pay in October, 1818. His London life as a man of letters was diversified by occasional visits to Paris. From 1834 to 1836 he was on military service in Spain, which provided him with the material for his *Movements of the British Legion* (1836). In 1838 he returned to Canada as correspondent of the *Times*. He found conditions such as to compel him, though it cost him his position, to advocate the cause of popular government. After about ten years in Canada, chiefly at Brockville, during which he failed to make an adequate income by journalistic, literary, and official work, he removed to New York. There, after a vain struggle to adapt his stories to a new group of readers and so make a living by his pen, and after even selling a much-loved dog in order to buy food, he died in poverty May 12, 1852, and lies in an unknown grave.

Richardson's imagination was early fired by his maternal grandfather's romantic tales of the Scottish Border and by his maternal grandmother's thrilling stories of events at Detroit in a way that reminds of the childhood of Scott. The novel and diversified environment of Richardson's childhood furnished further material for romantic narrative. To this were added the adventures of military life. Probably influenced by the work of Scott and Byron in the metrical romance, Richardson, as we have noticed in passing, cast his first narrative, *Tecumseh,* in poetic form, four cantos of *ottava rima.* Like Scott, Richardson turned from verse to prose as the medium for his romantic narratives, a course the wisdom of which may have been suggested also by the success of Cooper's early work.

In his first novel, *Ecarté,* imitative of Lytton's society novels, Richardson attains vividness of setting, but fails to achieve effective characterization or unity of plot. In his next novel, under the influence of Cooper's successful Indian fiction, he turned to the story of Pontiac, with the events and setting of which he was thoroughly familiar, and produced *Wacousta,* a great advance on its predecessor and, in spite of its faults, Richardson's masterpiece.

The faults are stilted dialogue, melodrama, and sensationalism. As some of these occur in other Canadian novelists, it may be well at this point to make clear what is meant by such of these terms as need explanation. Melodrama results when, in order to get striking serious situations, an author sacrifices probability in character drawing or in plot building. Sensationalism results when striking serious situations, probable or improbable, are over-elaborated. All of Richardson's outstanding faults are illustrated in the ninth chapter of *Wacousta,* the account of the execution of Reginald Halloway. Small as the amount of dialogue is, some of it seems unnatural. And certainly events and the character of De Haldimar are made to lack plausibility in

[75]

order that the execution may not be prevented. Even if character and plot had been handled in such a way as to make the execution seem inevitable, there would remain the element of sensationalism in the treatment. The presence of the coffin of the condemned man is presented to our imagination to the point of repulsion, and the way in which Ellen Halloway's body becomes covered and her clothing saturated with the blood of her husband is too horrible for readers of refined sensibilities, as is the later scene in which the same woman is made to grasp in her naked hands the unsheathed blade of a large knife which another woman is trying to take away from her. The careful reader will find no difficulty in detecting other examples of melodramatic and sensational writing in *Wacousta*. They are far more likely to occur in romantic fiction than in realistic, in the very nature of the circumstances, and people with a romantic taste of course take less notice of these faults than do people with a realistic taste.

Our recognition of the artistic weaknesses in *Wacousta* should not blind us to its merits. It is a very carefully constructed narrative filled with rapid action and vivid presentation of scenes, and it is rich in suspense, a quality dear to every taste in fiction.

After Richardson lost his position as correspondent of the *Times,* he continued his efforts in Canadian fiction in association with the *Literary Garland.* Some of the material which he contributed to this magazine he utilized in his *The Canadian Brothers* (1840), the setting of which is the period of the war of 1812 and the plot of which is linked with that of *Wacousta* by means of the curse of Ellen Halloway. The sequel, more melodramatic than its predecessor, plays up Canadian achievement in the war, and is thus highly significant as Richardson's response to the persistent demand for Canadian subjects as essential to a national literature, a response the patriotism of which heightens the pathos of his failure to live by his pen in Canada.

With Richardson's work in the romantic historical novel may be mentioned that of Rosanna Eleanor (Mullins) Leprohon (1832–79), a lifelong resident of Montreal, who was educated, as was Richardson's mother, at the Convent of the Congregation of Notre Dame. She began writing at fourteen, and while yet in her teens was one of the leading contributors to the *Literary Garland*. In 1851 she married Dr. J. L. Leprohon, Vice-consul for Spain. Without neglect of domestic, social, or religious duties, she continued to contribute prose and verse to periodicals in the United States and in Canada, and wrote novels. After a tedious illness she died, a relatively young woman.

In content her verse shows the influence of the English romantic movement. There are many echoes of the Graveyard School. Of a mystically religious nature, she based most of her poems dealing with the past on the Bible or on church history or tradition. Her humanitarianism is emotionally effective at times, even though it is occasionally the expression of a rather artificial Tennyson-like quarrel with difference of rank as a barrier between lovers. Her poems

[77]

of Canadian nature are her best. In these she comes nearest to freedom from her ever-present weaknesses, lack of metrical smoothness and of adaption of verse movement to lyric mood.

Her novels, constructed somewhat after the manner of French classical drama, with few characters and a simple plot, show some narrative skill. Four of them have been translated into French and have been equally popular with French- and English-Canadian readers. Historically, her novels are important because, from her residence in Montreal, she was able to re-create effectively the society of the French *Régime* and of the English Occupation, and because she was the first Canadian novelist whose work is the direct result of the nationalistic movement in Canadian literature.

CHAPTER 10

WILLIAM KIRBY
(1817–1906)

Kirby has been called the last of the Loyalists. As such he is only one special historic manifestation of a type common in British history. At the time when Charles I was in conflict with Parliament, this type took the Royal side. When the House of Stuart was divided against itself, this type espoused the Jacobite cause. In the days of the Loyalists, this type was characterized by Toryism and by intense devotion to the Anglican Church. In both these respects Kirby challenges comparison with Haliburton. Both had the same contempt for democratic principles in government, and Kirby had perhaps even a more devout regard for the established Church of England. He was not able, like Haliburton, to make the embodiment of his strong feelings his supreme literary expression. Rather, he depends for his fame on that part of his literary output that has the widest popular appeal.

Kirby's sentiments are not at all surprising when we consider his ancestry. On his father's side, he was descended from an old family, the Kirbys of Kirby Wiske, Yorkshire, England. This ancestral seat is made use of in two of the best poems in the author's *Canadian Idylls*. Although the family was relatively inconspicuous, its members were of the type on which depends the solidity of the British Empire. On his mother's side, Kirby was descended from the Watson family of Hull, some members of which were important enough in their time to have space accorded them in our biographical dictionaries, and three members of which, each named Thomas Watson, attempted literary work, one of the three being a sufficiently close friend of Spencer to be mourned by his superior brother craftsman under the name Amyntas.

William Kirby was born at Kingston-on-Hull, Yorkshire, England, October 13, 1817. While he was still a child, his parents emigrated to Cincinnati, Ohio. There he attended the school of a famous Scottish schoolmaster named Alexander Kinmont, and evidently received a sound classical education, for in addition to a good mastery of English, Latin, and French, he had also some command of German, Swedish, and Hebrew. After seven years in Cincinnati, spent partly at school and partly at work, the stirring of the Loyalist blood inherited from his great-grandmother, who had been driven back to England from Virginia by the Revolution, prompted Kirby to come to Canada, where he arrived in 1839. Although the rebellion of Mackenzie and Papineau had been put down, there was still the possibility of his having an opportunity to express in action his Loyalist sentiment, for the "Sympathisers" and the "Hunters' Lodges" were active on the United-States side of the border, and one of the objects of the agitators was to sever Canada from the British Empire, an object than which no other would more have aroused Kirby's blood to fighting pitch. Two other young men who were to have come to Canada with Kirby having found it impossible to do so, Kirby came alone, his entire baggage consisting of his wardrobe, his rifle, and a trunkful of classical books.

After visiting Niagara, Toronto, Montreal, Quebec, and again Montreal, Kirby decided, by tossing a coin, not to make his residence in Quebec, and returned to Niagara, the chief Loyalist settlement in Upper Canada (the older name was Newark). In Niagara he spent nearly all of the remaining days of his long but uneventful life, one of the most stirring incidents of which must have been his being in arms against the Fenians in 1867. In Niagara he was for twenty years editor and publisher of the *Mail,* a position which he resigned in 1871 to become, by the appointment of Sir John A. Macdonald, Collector of Customs at Niagara, an office which he held for twenty-four years. In 1882 he was one of the original Fellows of the Royal Society of Canada, from which he retired in 1894. He died June 23, 1906, in his eighty-ninth year. That he passed on to his descendants his strong sentiment of loyalty is shown by the fact that two of his grandsons served in the Great War, in which service one of them lost his life.

Kirby's first work of any importance in the history of Canadian literature is his *U.E. A Tale of Upper Canada.*

partly based on historical events in the Niagara district, written in 1846 and published in 1859; and its significance is more historical than artistic. In it are brought together the strands of immigration to Canada direct from the mother land and immigration by the Loyalist route. The poem tells of an English widower and his two sons, who, leaving a daughter and sister behind them in their ancestral Yorkshire home, reach Canadian shores after experiencing a severe storm at sea, sail up the St. Lawrence past many an historical place (specified in the poem), and reach their destination near Niagara. There they meet Ranger John, a Loyalist, and hear his account of his experiences in the period of the Revolution. From that time until the stormy days of 1837 and 1838 the poem blends the lives of the two families in one story, a sad aspect of which is the traitorous disloyalty of Ranger John's son Hugh.

Obviously there were epic possibilities in this material, and so we are not surprised to find that in form the poem shows classical influence by its division into twelve cantos, by Virgilian echoes, and by an apostrophe to Virgil; and neo-classical influence by the use of the heroic couplet of Pope's translated epics and of Goldsmith's *Deserted Village,* by descriptions of Canadian landscape and life idealized in the manner of Goldsmith, and by an apostrophe to Goldsmith. On the other hand, the descriptions of a tempest at sea and of a thunder-storm on land are distinctly Byronic, and the accounts of battle are reminiscent of Scott.

[82]

Important from the Canadian point of view are the expressions of regret for the dismemberment of the Anglo-Saxon world by the revolution and of patriotic fervour for Canada as a part of the Empire. In fact Canadian scenes are glorified not so much because they are things of beauty in themselves as because they constitute an ideal place in which to foster the British sentiments to which he was so intensely devoted.

Canadian Idylls (1888 and 1894), as the title, dedication, first motto, use of blank verse, and publication in instalments would lead one to expect, is decidedly Tennysonian in manner and method, especially in general resemblance to the *Idylls of the King*. Here, as also in the earlier volume, there is not the careful selection and arrangement of details that secure effective narrative. The later volume may be commended, however, for some good description of Canadian scenery, for the incidental picture of Canadian life in the fishermen's picnic which constitutes the framework of *The Queen's Birthday* and in "The Lord's Supper in the Wilderness", one of the constituent poems, and for the pride with which the author makes use of events from Canadian history.

A great deal better known than his poems are Kirby's prose works. His political writings belong to the field of journalism, and are not even of historical significance in the development of Canadian literature. Most of his other prose writings are of interest primarily to the general historian. The work by which Kirby is best known, and the one on which his lasting fame as an artist depends, is *The*

[83]

Golden Dog (1877). This novel can perhaps be best appreciated at its true worth by comparison with the earlier historical fiction of Richardson and with the later work of Parker in a similar vein. We have already noticed the methods of Richardson and the merits and defects of his accomplishment by these methods.

Like Richardson, Kirby sets his novel in a definite period of Canadian history. His sub-title is "A Romance of the Days of Louis Quinze in Quebec". He introduces some historical events and many historical characters, and makes free use of historical detail in the setting. Most striking of all is the historic tablet which gives the novel its main title. On the General Post Office in Quebec, above the door facing Montmorency Park, may be seen today the tablet of the golden dog. When Kirby visited Quebec in 1839 he saw this tablet on the façade of a large stone house on the Rue Buade. In 1865 he was again in Quebec and read Sir James M. LeMoine's story of the tablet and the stone house. (See "Maple Leaves", First Series, 1863, pp. 29–32). On the tablet, in addition to the figure of a dog in gold, are four lines of French, one above the figure and three below it, which, translated, read:—

I am a dog who is gnawing the bone;

While gnawing it, I am taking my repose.

A time will come which is not come

When I will bite who has bitten me.

In Kirby's novel, the house of the golden dog is owned by a Quebec merchant named Philibert, an historical character, who tries to protect the French Canadians from the thievery of Bigot and "The Grand Company", and who is a close rival of his son for the place of hero in the novel. The plot is elaborated by weaving together several complicated love stories, and the most selfish and scheming lovers, who will even stoop to murder, are contrasted with the most unselfish, in a manner dear to the hearts of all romanticists. With such a plot in such a setting and with the work of Richardson as an example, it would have been easy for Kirby, who obviously was a careful reader of the elder Dumas, to yield to the temptation to be melodramatic, a fault of which some critics have accused him.

This accusation, however, may be the result of the critics' confusing melodramatic with sensational writing. That Kirby does resort to sensationalism, that is, to over-elaboration of detail in scenes of violent action and intense emotion, may be readily admitted. But that he gets his strong situations by melodramatic devices, that is, by sacrificing probability of plot and truth of characterization, is by no means so certain. Rather, the intense situations are the plausible if not inevitable result of the forces at work in the lives of the characters. In fact, the great superiority of Kirby over Richardson is that by very careful attention to characterization Kirby approached decidedly more nearly than Richardson to that artistically ideal state in fiction in which the plot is what it is because the characters are what they are. To anticipate for a moment, if the reader finds Parker "thin" after having read Kirby first, the explanation, prob-

[85]

ably, lies in the richness of characterization in Kirby as contrasted with Parker's almost exclusive dependence upon the interest of plot. *The Golden Dog,* then, is important not only because of its successful use of native material, which undoubtedly influenced Parker to choose Canadian subject matter (in the use of which many believe he has done his best work), but also because of its excellent characterization and powerful dramatic scenes, which entitle it to consideration as the greatest Canadian novel.

CHAPTER II

SIR GILBERT PARKER
(1859–........)

Right Honourable Horatio Gilbert Parker is the most widely known of Canadian novelists. Three different dates are given by authorities as the year of his birth, 1859, 1860, and 1862. Whatever may be the year in which he was born, there is no doubt as to some of the important strains in his blood. His mother was of United Empire Loyalist descent. His father, born in Ireland of English parentage, was a captain in the Canadian militia, in which capacity he served in the suppression of the Rebellion of 1837. His son Gilbert, the eldest of six children, was born at Camden East, Lennox and Addington County, Ontario.

Young Parker was not blessed with robust health, and his physical condition no doubt tended to intensify his natural studiousness of temperament and eagerness for knowledge. This did not prevent him from cultivating an appreciation of nature by rambling in field and wood. He received part of his education by private instruction. Having passed through the schools of his birthplace, he attended the Ottawa

Normal School, from which he obtained a second-class teacher's certificate when he was seventeen years of age. He taught school for a while and then, having decided to take holy orders in the Church of England, entered Trinity College, Toronto. After two years at Trinity, he turned again to teaching, this time on the staff of the Ontario Institute for the deaf and dumb, at Belleville. He later attempted to serve the Church by taking a curacy at Trenton, Ontario. He soon resigned his charge there, perhaps because he already realized that his future lay with literature rather than with the Church. He took a summer course in oratory, taught that subject for a while at Queen's University, and acquired a reputation as an elocutionist. The state of his health, however, made it desirable if not necessary to seek a warmer climate.

In 1885 Parker left Canada and went to Australia, intending merely to make a tour of that country. On the completion of his tour, he was offered and he accepted the position of associate editor of the Sydney *Herald*. The offer provided opportunity not only to acquire experience in journalism, but also to travel, so that by the time Parker left Australia he had visited many parts of that continent and most of the islands of the South Seas.

In 1889, after nearly four years residence in Australia, Parker moved to London, and there, except for frequent visits to Canada and extensive travel throughout the Empire, he has since chiefly resided. In 1895 he married a wealthy New York woman named Van Tine, who, up to her death in 1925, was a great help to her husband in the achievement of literary success and of social distinction. Parker has been honoured with three doctor's degrees, a knighthood, a baronetcy, and election to Parliament and to the Privy Council. He organized the first Imperial Universities Conference, at London, England, in 1903. For eight years he was Chairman of the Imperial South African Association.

Circumstances of residence and travel have intensified Parker's native imperialism. As to his attitude to his native land, there are two opinions. Some think that he has toward Canada a snobbish attitude, bordering on contempt. Others think that, though he naturally prefers the refinements of upper-class English society to the rather pioneer conditions of a comparatively new country, he has a wholesome affection for the land of his birth. Whatever may be the truth in this matter, it is certain that he numbered among his friends some of the most distinguished residents of Canada, such as Sir John A. Macdonald, Sir Wilfrid Laurier, Sir Etienne Cartier, and Sir George R. Parkin, the last of whom we shall meet again as one of the shaping influences in the lives of Roberts and Carman. Parker also became a Fellow of the Royal Society of Canada.

From boyhood Parker could tell a good story. His appreciation of the dramatic is suggested by the reputation he had at Queen's of knowing Shakespeare by heart. As the result of a combination of circumstances, his early work was in the dramatic form. These are facts to be remembered in view of the strong dramatic situations in which his fiction

[89]

abounds. While in Australia, he praised in an anonymous article the acting of George Reynolds in Shakespeare's *Henry V*. So pleased was the actor with the article that he sought out the author, made his acquaintance, and induced him to try his hand at drama. Parker made a successful adaptation of *Faust* and wrote other plays. When he came to London, conditions were unfavourable to dramatists. As some members of his family were dependent on him, he could not afford to run the risk of financial failure in an adventure in the field of drama. He therefore turned his attention to non-dramatic prose fiction. He possessed in a high degree the sense for the romantically interesting in scene, character, and situation, a sense of the foremost importance in the successful writing of historical romance. By dint of native talent and extraordinary capacity for work, Parker soon became widely known as the author of historical romantic fiction of two types, tales and novels.

This does not mean that he neglected other forms of literature. He began to write verse at a comparativley early age, and he has published two volumes of poems. These include a sonnet sequence and many lyrics in other forms. A number of his lyrics have been set to music by eminent composers and sung by famous singers. He has also attracted favourable temporary notice at different periods of his life by his travel sketches and by his writings on current history. It is on his fiction, however, that his fame depends.

There is a story to the effect that on his return from Australia he showed a collection of tales to a then noted war correspondent, who told him he had the best collection of titles he had ever seen, whereupon Parker took his manuscripts home and burnt them. Be that as it may, Parker soon showed the reading public that he could write tales that had something good about them besides the titles. Six collections of his tales have been published, four volumes of which have a Canadian setting, and in some of which, such as the Canadian volume entitled *Pierre and his People,* the separate stories are somewhat linked by the recurrence of some of the same characters in different stories. The four volumes of Canadian tales are concerned with French-Canadian life and with the earlier and more modern life of the Canadian Northwest. Of the remaining two volumes of tales, one deals with life in Australia and the South Seas and the other with life in Egypt and the Soudan. In all of his short fiction Parker shows himself an adept at choosing the kind of situation that has the most effective popular appeal and that lends itself most readily to successful romantic treatment in the space at his disposal. He plays up physical suffering, such as results from flogging, wounding with weapons, or other forms of physical violence; heroic adventure; sacrifice; magnanimous forgiveness of great injustice. In his use of striking situations, he is at times reminiscent of himself; in fact, his shorter fiction offers a good opportunity for a study of repetition of plots. Other characteristics of his tales, common also to the novels, will be noticed in connection with the latter.

[91]

His novels are set over an even wider geographical area than his short pieces of fiction, and in some cases the scene shifts in the same novel from one part of the British Empire to another. Of the novels with interests and setting of such Imperial scope, the best are: *The Weavers,* a novel of Egypt, in which the plot reflects the influence of Egyptian, British, and international politics; and *The Judgment House,* a work of even greater imaginative power and scope, the scene of which is partly London and partly South Africa.

Some characteristics, as we have implied in passing, are common to the tales and the novels. In both, the settings are strikingly vivid because, by visiting the actual scenes, Parker has enabled himself to give full play to his native powers of keen observation and felicitous description In both, he is a master at creating suspense, in exposition, he occasionally plays up physical suffering, sometimes to the point of being sensational, sometimes perhaps even to the point of being melodramatic. In both, the characters are re-membered, not for the skill with which they are represented, but for the striking situations in which the author has placed them. In both, the scenes are laid in almost every section of the British Empire.

The wide geographical distribution of his settings gives him some opportunities in the novel that do not offer them-selves in the shorter fiction. In several of the novels set in some particular part of the Empire, he greatly broadens his range of appeal by introducing in a highly dramatic manner some subject of great Imperial importance, so as to attract readers all over the Empire. In this way a story set in Egypt or South Africa can be made to have intense interest for a Canadian reader.

All fiction written with so perfect a knowledge of the romancer's craft is bound to be widely appreciated, whether or not it is high in artistic quality. From the point of view of Canadian readers certainly, and perhaps also from the point of view of readers outside of Canada, Parker's best work, in both short pieces of fiction and romantic novels, is that in which, following the lead of Kirby and others, he makes Canadian characters, historical or imagined, or both, enact the events of the romantic plot in a more or less realistic Canadian setting.

Of the Canadian novels, two are of special romantic interest; *When Valmond Came to Pontiac* because it brings the Napoleonic legend to a remote village in Quebec, and *The Right of Way* because it presents a fascinating study in abnormal psychology. From the artistic point of view, the most important of Parker's Canadian novels, and perhaps of all his novels, is *The Seats of the Mighty,* a novel of the conquest of Canada. The setting of this novel at once suggests comparison with Kirby's *The Golden Dog.* Many readers of taste will find Parker's novel "thin" after having previously read *The Golden Dog.* The reason is not far to seek. Parker, like all romanticists, works for striking situations. But he does not characterize with anything like the subtle finish that distinguishes Kirby's novel in addition to

[93]

its striking romantic situations. In estimating the artistic quality of a novel, we must consider plot, setting, and character, and of these the greatest is character. Therefore *The Seats of the Mighty,* notwithstanding its points of excellence, is not a serious rival to *The Golden Dog* for the honour of being the greatest Canadian novel.

CHAPTER 12

OTHER NOVELISTS, HISTORICAL AND REGIONAL

It may seem strange at first thought to consider together historical and regional novelists. A moment's reflection, however, will show that such a grouping is justifiable. In the course of time regional novels that are good enough to survive acquire historical significance, and they may be even more trustworthy in this respect than historical novels, because the use of fact in the latter is based largely on research, whereas in the former it is based on the author's first-hand observation.

Of the Canadian authors of historical and regional fiction other than those previously considered, some, such as Miss Machar, Lighthall, Marquis, Theodore Goodridge Roberts, and Mrs. McClung, are adequately treated in the handbooks. Others, such as Miss Saunders and C. G. D. Roberts, will be discussed in connection with the fields in which the major portion of their work lies. Here we shall consider "Basil" King, Arthur Stringer, "Marian Keith", "Ralph Connor", and L. M. Montgomery.

[95]

Some people question the appropriateness of including King and Stringer in the list of Canadian authors in that they both moved to the United States and to a large extent used American material and shaped it to suit American tastes. But both are Canadian born and both have set fiction in definite Canadian localities. Moreover, as Stringer has said, speaking of his boyhood: "the gun is loaded then, and what you may bring down when you are forty or fifty is determined by what you've loaded it with when you were five or ten."

William Benjamin King (1859–1928), who wrote under the name Basil King, was born at Charlottetown, Prince Edward Island, and attended St. Peter's School there, after which he went to Windsor, Nova Scotia, then the seat of the University of King's College, from which he obtained his master's degree in due course. He was for several years rector of St. Luke's Cathedral, Halifax, later taking charge of Christ Church, Cambridge, Massachusetts. He married an American woman and made his permanent residence in the United States for the rest of his days. Not only has he introduced Canadian characters into some of his American fiction, but he set one novel, *In the Garden of Charity* (1903), on the South shore of Nova Scotia long before Norwood set his narrative poem *Bill Boram* there, or "Connor" and Frank Parker Day their novels *Treading the Winepress* and *Rockbound* respectively, and King will not suffer from a comparison with the others in the way of artistic handling of his material.

[96]

Arthur Stringer (1874–........) was born at London, Ontario. There, as part of a thoroughly normal boyhood, he attended the public school and the collegiate institute, after which he attended University College, Toronto, and Oxford for one academic year, spent some time in travel, and engaged for a while in journalism, first in Montreal and then in New York. Since moving to New York he has lived temporarily on a fruit farm in Ontario and on a wheat farm in the foothills of Alberta. His experience on the latter farm furnished him with the background for the work that best entitles him to consideration in a study of Canadian literature, namely, the trilogy consisting of *The Prairie Wife* (1916), *The Prairie Mother* (1919), and *The Prairie Child* (1921).

This trilogy is the story of a woman who is the product of the cultured East of this continent and who thinks that love is enough to make her happy, even though the reader may foresee difficulty in that her husband is not capable of sharing her refined tastes and in that she will be cut off in her new prairie home from most of the amenities of civilization to which she has been accustomed. The first volume presents her life immediately after marriage. The second records the events centering around the birth and infancy of her first child. The third traces the early years of this child and the gradual estrangement of the parents. Though the series may give the impression of artificiality, of being made to order, the prairie background is vividly sketched,

[97]

and the clash of wills among the characters frequently furnishes tensely dramatic situations.

Even if Stringer had not written this trilogy in a Canadian setting, he would have some claim for recognition as a Canadian author in that his *Lonely O'Malley* (1901), is a classic of Canadian boyhood, as *Tom Sawyer* and *Huckleberry Finn* are classics of American boyhood.

"Marian Keith", who was born at Rugby, Ontario, and whose maiden name was Mary Esther Miller, was educated at Orillia High School and Toronto Normal School. After teaching school for a while, she married Reverend Donald C. MacGregor, then stationed at Orillia, Ontario. She has received adequate recognition in the handbooks for her regional fiction, but not for her historical novel, *A Gentleman Adventurer* (1924), the dedication of which is signed from London, Ontario. From the first sentence to the last this book is an example of narrative art on a very high level. The gentleman adventurer and his lady are the stuff of which romances are made, and they are presented in a very romantic historical setting, their love story culminating synchronously with the Riel Rebellion. Though plot, setting, and characters are thus highly romantic, every situation is adequately prepared for, so that the novel produces a very decided impression of reality. One of the finest qualities of the book is the art with which the author shows the influence of spiritual forces in shaping character and destiny. This novel deserves a permanent place among the historical novels of Canada.

[98]

Reverend Charles William Gordon (1860–........), widely known by his pen name, "Ralph Connor", was born in Glengarry County, Ontario, the son of a Presbyterian clergyman. He is a graduate of the University of Toronto and of Knox College, Toronto, and studied for a while at Edinburgh University. Several years of pioneer missionary work among the lumbermen and miners of the Canadian Northwest, especially in the Rocky Mountain districts, furnished him with part of the material later used in his numerous Western stories. For more than thirty-five years he has been pastor of St. Stephen's Church, Winnipeg, publishing novels as frequently as his professional, social, and civic duties will permit, too frequently in fact to produce works of artistic finish. An earnest preacher always, a fair artist sometimes, he is one of the three or four Canadian authors who have been most widely read in the English-speaking world. In addition to his Western novels, of which the earliest are decidedly the best, and the novel of the South Shore of Nova Scotia previously mentioned, he has written two novels of the Glengarry district in Ontario, so that his contribution to regional fiction has been quantitatively large. Whether or not his works would survive on their artistic merits alone, it seems highly probable that some of them, *Black Rock* and *The Sky Pilot* for example, will live because of their historical significance. In *The Runner* (1929) he attempted the historical novel proper. The action centres in the Niagara district during the stormy days of 1812-15. The title figure is a demi-god of British and French extraction, René La-

Flamme, who, as a "runner", in the service of Brock until the General's death, performs such feats of ingenuity, valour, and physical prowess as make glad the heart of the romantic reader, and keeps it up through nearly five hundred pages, to be rewarded in the end by the love of Charlotte Brookes.

The regionalists make a more or less natural transition from the romantic historical novelists to the realists that remain to be considered, and of all the regionalists perhaps none makes a better connecting link than L. M. Montgomery (1874–........). She was born at Clifton, Prince Edward Island, whence, in her early infancy, the family moved to Cavendish. After attending the district school there until she was sixteen years of age, she spent a year each at Prince of Wales College, Charlottetown, and Dalhousie University, Halifax, Nova Scotia. In 1911 she married Rev. Ewan Macdonald and moved to Leaskdale, Ontario, where she spent about thirteen years before moving to Norval, Ontario.

She inherited with her Scottish blood a strain of poetry, and has written nature verse, particularly of the sea, characterized by play of fancy rather than by descriptive vividness. There is a deeper poetry of life in her verse. Her philosophy of fiction is well expressed by Mr. Carpenter in *Emily's Quests.* "Remember—pine woods are just as real as —pigsties—and a darn sight pleasanter to be in . . . And don't tell the world — everything. That's what's the mattter — with our — literature. Lost the charm of mystery — and reserve." In all of her fiction, especially in her treatment of a child life, by throwing "a certain colouring of imagination" over the humour and pathos of the incidents of common life as lived in a picturesque rural environment, she achieves a rare combination of truth and beauty that may best be described as poetic realism.

Her most important short stories, published in two volumes, show a fine sense for the story values in single tragic or comic incidents or episodes in common life and for idyllic settings. As a novelist she is distinctive among the authors of regional fiction in that she usually links her novels in series by continuing the story of important characters. *Kilmeny of the Orchard, The Blue Castle,* and *Magic for Marigold* are not linked with any others, though the last, just out (1929), may well be, for it is an idyllic treatment of the childhood of Marigold Lesley that compares favourably with the Anne and Emily books, of which the series consist of six and three respectively.

The Anne series is a *comédie humaine* unparalleled in Canadian fiction. *Anne of Green Gables* is a fascinating story of the childhood and young girlhood of a remarkably sensitive and highly original character in the home into which she has been adopted. *Anne of Avonlea* widens her sphere from the home to the community by making her the village schoolmistress. *Anne of the Island* shows the heroine reflecting glory on her native province by her distinctive work in college. The last three books of the series give us glimpses of Anne's life as a woman. She marries her former schoolmate, now Dr. Gilbert Blythe, has six children, and experiences the tragedy of the Great War. Though the interest shifts largely to the children, the mother's personality exerts an important influence throughout the series. To write such a series is a notable literary achievement.

The Emily series shows an improvement over the Anne series in that there is a more logical relation between character and plot. Not only is the plot what it is because the people are what they are, but also we know why the people are what they are: the relation between character and heredity and environment is so clearly traced that the books of the series, individually and collectively, produce the impression of organic unity.

A reading of *The Blue Castle,* an adventure in romantic fiction for adults that makes idyllic use of the Muskoka country as a setting, will convince the student of L. M. Montgomery's works that her future fame depends upon her stories of children.

CHAPTER 13

SOME RECENT NOVELISTS

The preceding discussions by no means exhaust the subject of Canadian historical and regional fiction. A few more names will suggest the vitality that is continuously manifest in these fields. Three Canadianized Scots, Bertrand William Sinclair (1878–........), Robert Watson (1882–........), and Frederick William Wallace (1886–........), have written colourful fiction. Sinclair has written effectively of mountain, forest, and sea in British Columbia, his *Poor Man's Rock* (1920) depicting the life of the salmon fishermen of the Pacific Coast and his *Hidden Places* (1922) vividly describing the experiences of the lumbermen. Watson has used as setting for his stories various parts of Western Canada, including the Pacifiic Coast and the Arctic. Wallace became specially interested in the Atlantic fisheries and wrote *The Viking Blood* (1921), *Blue Water* (1924), and *Captain Salvation* (1925) as a result. The seafaring life of Nova Scotians has been vividly depicted also by Frank Parker Day *(The Autobiography of a Fisherman* (1927) and *Rockbound* (1928))* and by Arthur Hunt

[103]

Chute (1888–1929). Day has also pictured life on the Churchill River, purely from imagination, in his *River of Strangers* (1926). Other novelists of British Columbia and the Pacific Coast, besides Sinclair, are Isabel Ecclestone Mackay (1875–1928), Robert Allison Hood, and Percy Gomery.

In general the historical and regional novelists have emphasized romance and adventure, although there is a tendency toward realism in Stringer's prairie trilogy, in Sinclair's novels of the salmon fishermen and the lumbermen of British Columbia, and in all of Day's regional fiction. But the greatest novels of all lands have been the work of the realists, and Canada, too, must depend on her realists to produce fiction that will compare favourably with the greatest fiction of other countries. Canada has had a beginning of what promised to be a realistic school, and the most significant names in this connection are Robert James Campbell Stead (1880–........), Mazo de la Roche (1885–........), Laura (Goodman) Salverson, and Frederick Philip Grove (1872–........).

Stead's parents were natives of Lanark, Ontario, and he was born at Middleville, near Lanark. The family moved to Manitoba in 1882, and so Stead was educated in Manitoba. In 1895 he took a position as clerk in a store. From 1898 to 1910 he published *The Review,* at Cartwright, Manitoba, and from 1908-9 *The Courier,* at Crystal City, Manitoba. In 1910 he went to Alberta, where he was in the automobile business between the years 1910 and 1912, was on the editorial staff of the Calgary *Albertan,* 1912-13, and began the publicity work for the Canadian Pacific Railway which ultimately resulted in his taking residence at Ottawa in 1919 as Director of Publicity, Department of Immigration and Colonization. His experience in journalism and publicity work was excellent preparation for fiction.

From the point of view of the present discussion Stead's work is significant for its truthful representation of the West. Persons of taste who are nauseated with the unreality of "Western stories" of the ordinary type will be gratified to find in Stead something different, something that rings true even if one has never been so fortunate as to have personal experience of the West. The novels in which his realism, his descriptive power, and his vigorous, rapid style are best exemplified are *Neighbours* (1922), *The Smoking Flax* (1924), and *Grain* (1927).

Mazo de la Roche (1885–........) was born in Toronto, of French, Irish, and English descent, the de la Roches having been French Royalists who took refuge in Ireland at the time of the French Revolution. In the city of her birth she attended public school, the Parkdale Collegiate, the University of Toronto, and the College of Art. The acceptance of a story caused her to give up the idea of becoming a black-and-white illustrator and to turn to literature as a profession. Toronto has remained her permanent residence, but she spends happy hours at her summer cottage on Lake Ontario, and since winning the *Atlantic Monthly* prize for *Jalna,* she has participated in the pleasures of travel.

Her achievement with *Jalna* has tended to overshadow her most artistic accomplishment in the Canadian novel. Her right to a high place in Canadian realistic fiction depends, up to the present, on one novel only, *Possession* (1923). Before this her work had been characterized by Dickensian whimsical and fantastic humour in depicting child life rather than by verisimilitude, as will be realized from a reading of *Explorers of the Dawn* (1922), a book the material of which had been previously published in periodicals. In *Possession* she wrote an excellent realistic Canadian novel, the action of which centres round a fruit farm in Ontario. The setting is very colourfully presented, especially as it is affected by the annual arrival of Indians to help pick the fruit. Moreover, plot, setting, and character are organically interrelated so as to produce a very decided impression of artistic unity. The novel aroused great but as yet unrealized expectations as to the author's possible contribution to realistic Canadian fiction.

Delight (1926), as the names of the heroine, Delight Mainprize, and of other characters suggest, is somewhat in the author's Dickensian vein. In it she occasionally slips from reality, and in the Jalna books *(Jalna* (1927) and *Whiteoaks of Jalna* (1929)*)* she falls with a crash so far as writing realistic Canadian fiction is concerned. It is true that the Jalna material is set in Canada and that this affords the author an opportunity to use her descriptive powers, but otherwise the setting might almost as well be Kamchatka or Zanzibar, for it does not affect the story in any noticeable organic way. Moreover, the characters behave neither like human beings in general nor like English people settled in Canada in particular.

The fact of the matter is that the Jalna books are a triumph of journalistic rather than of literary art. Journalistic art seeks the extraordinary, the unusual, the bizarre, the freakish, the eccentric, and is at its best when its subject is unique; literary art, especially in realistic fiction, seeks the typical, the representative, and at its best attains to universality. Significantly enough, the reviews of the Jalna books by professional journalists have been very enthusiastic — the winning of a ten-thousand-dollar prize is in itself a fact of great journalistic importance. Whether Miss de la Roche's natural gift is, as her plays and most of her novels indicate, for the whimsical and the fantastic and her success in realism a happy accident, or whether she is by nature a realistic artist temporarily sidetracked at Jalna, only time will tell. For the present it may be said that her most heralded achievement is journalism glorified and that *Possession* is her most artistic work in the novel.

Another woman who, up to the present, has increased the sum of excellent Canadian realistic fiction by only one novel is Laura (Goodman) Salverson, born in Winnipeg, in the early nineties, of Icelandic descent. Despite a youth of vicissitude, she found adequate stimulus and literary background for the development of her artist's temperament through her mother's culture and her father's love of books. Her quick intelligence and keen insight compensated in large measure for the meagreness of her formal education. She has lived at Duluth, Minnesota, Regina, Saskatchewan, and Calgary, Alberta, her present home.

Encouraged by favourable comment on her verse, of which she later published a volume, and by the winning of a prize for a short story, she wrote in three months, and published in the year that *Possession* appeared, her contribution to Canadian realistic fiction, *The Viking Heart* (1923). With compelling realism and yet with unusual poetic charm, she weaves her story of the joys and sorrows, the victories and defeats, the comedies and tragedies of several Icelandic families in rural Manitoba and in the city of Winnipeg. Genuinely epic is the narrative of the struggles by which the Icelandic immigrants, rich only in the possession of the Viking heart, rise from their pioneer poverty to positions in which they are able to make a definite contribution to the welfare of Canada, now their country.

As to her subsequent novels, *When Sparrows Fall* (1925) makes use of her American experience, and *Lord of the Silver Dragon* (1927) is an epic of the Norsemen in the time of Leif Ericson. Whether she will give us more realistic Canadian fiction like *The Viking Heart* is for the future to reveal.

The most important name in Canadian realistic fiction, if not in the whole field of the Canadian novel, is Frederick Philip Grove (1872–........). Grove was born in Europe, of Swedish and Scottish parentage. He travelled widely as a young man, making visits to all parts of Europe and to most parts of the world, included in which was a scientific expedition to South America. In the nineties he had literary associations in London with groups of which H. G. Wells and Wilde were members. He visited Canada in 1892, and came there, to stay, in 1894. The vicissitudes of his life in Canada and the United States before he established himself as a teacher in Manitoba, are well represented in *A Search for America* (1927), considered in the discussion of autobiography. He is a graduate of the University of Manitoba. The keenness and discernment of his study of literature is suggested by the material in *It needs to be said* (1929). He has been writing for approximately thirty years, — novels, sketches, poems,—but has published sparingly.

To appreciate fully his work as a realistic novelist, one needs to know his descriptive pieces, *Over Prairie Trails* (1922) and *The Turn of the Year* (1923). The key to the distinctiveness of his descriptive writing is found in his careful reading of such English naturalists as Belt and Darwin and such American naturalists as Audubon, Thoreau, and Burroughs and in his own practice: ' "Observing" means to me as much finding words to express what I see as it means the seeing itself.' He can write on the one hand with such objectivity as to create a rhetorical paradox, literary scientific description, and on the other hand with such subjectivity as to fuse the thing described, the describer, and the rest of the universe into an harmonious cosmic unit. As

a literary recorder of the seasonal and atmospheric phenomena of the Canadian prairies he stands supreme.

His novel *Settlers of the Marsh* (1925) revealed him
as probably the supreme interpreter in fiction of Canadian
prairie life, and no other aspect of Canadian life has been
better done, if it has ever been done as well. Grove's novel
is, moreover, a profound treatment of sexual love, a fact that
the vicious prudery still prevalent in some parts of Canada
cannot permanently keep from being recognized. *Our Daily
Bread* (1928) is another magnificent study of prairie life,
about the realism of which the only serious critical question
that may be raised is whether it is not too sombre and bitter.
Be that as it may, the fiction of Grove is the most serious
rival of *The Golden Dog* for the supreme place in Canadian
fiction.

Chapter 14

NATURE WRITERS I — WRITERS OF ANIMAL STORIES

Nature in Canada is infinitely rich in variety and beauty, as those who are not fortunate enough to be able to travel widely in the Dominion may realize in a marked degree by reading Wilfred Campbell's *Canada*. The literary possibilities of Canadian nature have been incidentally suggested in the presentation of the settings of historical and regional Canadian novels. Canadian nature as the primary theme of the literary artist is found in two important types of writing, namely, descriptions of nature in general and stories of animal life in particular. In this discussion we are concerned with the latter.

Interest in animals is one of the oldest characteristics of mankind. The worship of animals, still a part of some of the Oriental religions, was an almost universal phase of religion in the most primitive stages of human development. Animals were worshipped because they were a source of fear or of mystery or because, according to the doctrine of transmigration of souls, they might house the souls of men.

Nearly every animal, at some time in some place by some group of people, has been the object of worship.

The interest in animals as objects of worship may have helped to give rise to the use of animals as characters in stories that have a moral significance. Be that as it may, the animal story is of very ancient origin, and it was widely prevalent in Europe during the middle ages. In it the animals are given human faculties, each animal or class of animal may embody a single human trait, and the story may be told primarily for the purpose of teaching men a lesson. Most fables, for example, are animal stories of this kind. The fable had its origin in remote antiquity, and the oldest fables that we have in their original form came from Hindustan. From there the form passed in time to China, Tibet, Persia, and Greece. Latin versions of fables were handed down to modern Europe, different nations of which have had original fabulists, and the tradition is vital in the New World today, as witness Joel Chandler Harris' re-telling, in negro dialect, of the Bre'r Rabbit and Uncle Remus stories and Ernest Thompson Seton's *Wood Myth and Fable*.

In modern times the interest in animals has been tremendously increased by the discoveries of science. The establishment of the theory of evolution led man to recognize the lower animals as his "kindred", and the study of the mental life of animals became important not merely as a fascinating subject in itself but also as a valuable source of information on some of the problems of human psychology. This great interest in animals prepared the way for the success of a new type of animal story, in the creation of which Canada has had a lion's share.

The animal stories by Canadian authors, whether written of "the kindred of the wild" or of domesticated animals, may be divided into three classes: those in which obviously no attempt is made to be true to animal psychology, the sole purpose being to tell a good story; those in which the authors aimed to be realistic but the semblance of reality is somewhat diminished by the feeling that the animals approach too nearly the human in their psychology; those in which the impression of reality is intensified by the seeming scientific accuracy of the animal psychology. The animal stories of Mrs. Traill have been already noticed in passing. Those of C. G. D. Roberts, the poet laureate of the animal world, will be considered in our study of his work in general. In this discussion we are concerned with Margaret Marshall Saunders, William Alexander Fraser, Ernest Thompson Seton, and Archie P. McKishnie.

Miss Saunders (1861-........) was born at Milton, Nova Scotia. As the daughter of a well-known Baptist minister, Edward Manning Saunders, she had more than one place of abode, and thus came to know life in the Annapolis Valley, as well as in the city of Halifax, where her father was for a time pastor of the First Baptist Church. Her early education was largely in the hands of her father. She began Latin at eight years of age. At fifteen she went to Trafalgar House School, Edinburgh, Scotland, and later continued her education at Orleans, France. On her return she engaged for a while in teaching school, and then spent more time in travel. She has travelled extensively in the United States as well as in Europe. At present Toronto is her place of residence. In 1929 she attended the meeting of the Canadian Authors Association at Halifax, and subsequently visited various places in Nova Scotia.

She has written a considerable amount of short fiction in addition to her novels. Her novels belong to two classes according to whether the interest is chiefly in human characters or in animal characters. In the former class are included a romance of the sea, *My Spanish Sailor* (1889), and a historical-regional romance, *Rose à Charlitte* (1898), published also under the title *Rose of Acadie,* a charming tale of life among the Acadians in Digby County, Nova Scotia. Her greatest achievement, however, is in her romances of animal life, in which human beings are presented as the animals see them. Her work in this field has covered a wide range, as the following list indicates: *Beautiful Joe* (1894), the autobiography of a dog, which has been translated into several languages and of which upwards of a million copies have been sold; *Beautiful Joe's Paradise* (1902), *Nita,* story of an Irish setter (1904), *Princess Sukey,* story of a pigeon and her human friends (1905), *Alpatok,* story of an Eskimo dog (1906), *My Pets* (1908), *Pussy Black-Face* (1913), *The Wandering Dog* (1916), *Golden Dickie,* the story of a canary and his friends (1919), *Bonnie Prince Fetlar,* the story of a pony and his friends (1920), *Jimmy Gold-coast* (1924), in which the title figure is a monkey, who associates with other interesting animal characters. Though people enjoy these stories as fascinating excursions into the land of romance rather than as realistic representations of animal psychology, nevertheless they find in them the close observation and imaginative insight of one who has spent a lifetime in the sympathetic study of animals.

W. A. Fraser (1859-........) was born at River John, Pictou County, Nova Scotia. He spent his early life in the United States and received his early education in New York and West Brooklyn. As a mining engineer he spent seven years in India, and five years in the Canadian West in the employ of the Federal Government. He later moved to Toronto, his present home.

He has written some poetry, and his varied experience has been a fruitful source of material for fiction. His collections of tales with human characters, graphic in setting and replete with thrilling situations attained (perhaps sometimes with the sacrifice of plausibility) by emphasis upon physical action, are occasionally like Parker's Pierre tales in dealing with frontier life in Western Canada and in being linked throughout a volume by a common character.

His animal stories are of three kinds. In the first, as in *Mooswa* (1900), he writes of Canadian animals in their habitat somewhat in the manner of Roberts and Seton. He does not describe the surroundings of the animals as vividly as Roberts does, nor does he give the impression of scientific accuracy that one gets from reading Seton, but he effectively

[115]

presents the action in which his animal characters are involved. A second kind of animal story by Fraser, as in *Thoroughbreds* (1902), and *Brave Hearts* (1904), treats vividly, sympathetically, and sometimes humorously, the life of the racehorse. In this, his own peculiar field, Fraser has done excellent work. The third kind of animal story written by Fraser is that found in the collection entitled *The Sa'-Zada Tales* (1905). In these tales the animals at the zoo tell their stories to each other and to the keeper, Sahib Zada. The vividness of these tales and the intimate knowledge of animal life that they display indicate that the author while in the Orient made a careful study of Oriental animals in their habitat. From the Canadian point of view, the most important of Fraser's animal stories are those of the first type.

Ernest Thompson Seton (1860-........), descended from a Scottish earl named Seton, whence the author's present surname, was born Thompson at South Shields, Durham County, England. He came to Canada at the age of five, and lived in the backwoods from 1866 to 1870. After attending the public schools of Toronto, he studied art from 1879 to 1881 at the Royal Academy, London, England. Subsequently he went to Manitoba to follow natural history, became government naturalist of that province, and spent the years from 1882 to 1887 on the prairies. From 1890 to 1896 he studied art in Paris. In 1899 he began lecturing on wild animals. In 1902 he started the Woodcraft Indians as an outdoor-life movement. His present home is Greenwich, Connecticut.

As a result of his work as government naturalist of Manitoba, he published two scientific works, *Mammals of Manitoba* (1886), and *Birds of Manitoba* (1891). His literary work deals chiefly with animals and outdoor life. His stories of animal life, apart from the fact that in a few of the earlier ones the animals were made to talk, show his scientific accuracy of observation, his insight into animal psychology, his humane sympathy, and his artistic imagination. He has been accused of humanizing too much the mental processes of his animals, rather a presumptuous charge, as very few have had similar opportunity for accurate observation or have been so willing to make the most of the opportunity. It is true, as he himself tells us, that the events in the life of a particular imagined animal may be a composite of events from the lives of several actual animals, but any literary artist has the right to do this, whether his characters are animal or human, so long as the character thus imagined is typical or representative. Seton's artistic imagination supplemented the knowledge of observation and moulded it into stories that are excellent from a literary point of view. His vivid word painting, accompanied by artistic illustrations (chiefly the work of the author, sometimes assisted by his wife), presents very graphically the setting and action of his animal fiction.

Archie P. McKishnie (1878-........), born at New Scotland, Ontario, is a younger brother of Mrs. Jean Blewett, and, like her, inherited from his mother a strain of Gaelic poetic blood. Their parents were both natives of Argyllshire. McKishnie was educated at Ridgetown and Toronto. His first literary position was the dramatic editorship of the *Toronto Sunday World*. After doing other editorial work, he became a free-lance writer, and now conducts courses of instruction in the writing of fiction.

He has written verse, short stories, and historical and contemporary fiction of novel length, in addition to his animal stories. It is in the last, however, that his literary qualities, including his gift for poetic phrase, are at their best, as a reading of *Openway* (1923), and *Mates of the Tangle* (1924), will clearly demonstrate. In the skill with which he presents his material, especially in the poetic description of the settings of his stories, he comes nearer than any other to being the peer of Roberts, which is indeed high praise.

Chapter 15

NATURE WRITERS II — LOCAL COLOURISTS

Several of the types of literature already studied contain incidental description of varying degrees of excellence. The memoirs and the literature of travel and exploration, for example, abound in descriptive passages. In historical and regional fiction and in animal stories, where the setting must be vividly presented, the service of description as the handmaid of narration is of more than usual importance. Writings of this kind make comparatively easy the transition to descriptive literature, in which description is not of secondary but of primary importance, and the writers of which have a more or less consciously formulated technique. Strictly speaking, not all descriptive writers are local colourists. Local-colour writing describes places and people in such a way as to bring out their peculiar characteristics. But no one can be a good local colourist in particular unless he is first a good descriptive artist in general. In this study we shall consider not merely local-colour writing in the strict sense of the term but Canadian literature in general in which the descriptive element is predominant. It therefore becomes necessary to learn what the descriptive writer can do for the reader and how he does it.

In the first place, the descriptive writer, like any other literary artist, can enable the reader to experience at second-hand what he may find it inconvenient or impossible to experience at first hand. Conditions that existed in the past but have now ceased to exist may be preserved for us in the pages of description handed down to us by people who lived in the midst of the vanished scene. The remote in place as well as in time may come to us in this way. Many people, for example, are in circumstances that do not permit them to see Niagara Falls with their own eyes and to hear its mighty roar with their own ears. Many such, however, have experienced Niagara Falls in imagination through descriptions of it in Canadian verse or prose. When we consider the number of objects, scenes, and persons that must be experienced in this way or not at all, we realize the tremendous value of good descriptive writing.

In the second place, we often need the descriptive artist even when we have been able to enjoy experience at first hand. Many people may be able to visit Niagara Falls no more than once. They may then be able to recall the experience by the unaided effort of their own imagination, and so experience repeatedly at second-hand what they experienced once at first hand. In most cases, however, such imaginative recalling of the original experience will be very

noticeably stimulated and intensified by the reading of a good
description of the same experience by some other person.

Even to people who can experience objects at first hand
as often as they choose, the descriptive artist may be of
service. In "Fra Lippo Lippi" Browning says:

> "For, don't you mark? we're made so that we love
> First when we see them painted, things we have passed
> Perhaps a hundred times nor cared to see;
> .... Art was given for that;
> God uses us to help each other so,
> Lending our minds out."

Though Browning was speaking specifically of painting, it
is the same when things are painted in words, by the descriptive artist. Art intensifies and clarifies because the artist
not only takes in with his keener senses what ordinary ob-
servers miss, but also expresses it in such a way that people
of normal responsiveness cannot fail to recognize it in art
though they have missed it in actuality. Who, for example,
would not have intensified his appreciation of nature in general by reading Wordsworth or of Canadian nature by reading Roberts and Lampman?

What does the descriptive writer do in order to accom-
plish these things for the reader and how does he do it?
An author describes his subject for one or both of two good
reasons: to enable his readers to experience indirectly through
imagination what he experiences directly through his senses,
especially the sense of sight; to create in his readers the mood

that the thing described created in him. If he describes for the first reason only, he is writing pictorial description, which may be either impressionistic, that is, sketched in broad general outline, or very specific in detail. If he describes for the second reason only, he is writing atmospheric description. In good descriptive material of any length, there is usually opportunity for both pictorial and atmospheric writing.

Whether the writing is to be pictorial or atmospheric or both, the language must be concrete. The means to concreteness of language are literal comparisons, figures of speech, and imagery, and in description imagery is of fundamental importance, as will become clear from a consideration of the nature of imagery, which it is the primary function of imagination to produce. Imagination in its basic aspect is the power of calling to mind absent objects which we have formerly experienced by one or more of the five senses. Since most people recall most easily and vividly objects experienced by the sense of sight, the word *image,* which originally meant a mental picture only, has been extended in meaning to include a mental impression of any kind of sense experience. Thus we have, according to the five senses, visual, auditory, gustatory (or palatal), olfactory, and tactile images. If we hear, read, or think the word *orange,* for example, we may have images of sight, touch, smell, and taste, because on some prior occasion we have experienced an actual orange with these four senses. We should not have an image of sound, because actual oranges do not ordinarily make any noise. Words like *choir, orchestra,* and *quartette,* however, suggest auditory images perhaps more promptly than they do visual ones.

Now suppose a descriptive writer wishes to enable his readers to experience in imagination a landscape that they cannot conveniently see for themselves. He cannot present the actual landscape, but he can present the words that stand for the different objects and aspects of objects as they appear in the landscape, and the readers, by putting these together, get a mental picture of the landscape as a whole, somewhat after the manner in which they would get a complete picture by putting together the separated parts of a picture puzzle. The words that stand for objects and aspects of objects are images. In description, the visual images naturally predominate, but many descriptions are made more vivid by the use of other kinds of images along with the visual images. Good imagery depends largely on the skill with which the writer chooses his adjectives, nouns, verbs, and adverbs. The more specific a noun or verb is, and the more carefully chosen the adjective or adverb, respectively, that modifies it, the more easily, and hence the more vividly, will readers experience in imagination the subject on which the descriptive writer is exercising his art, whether he chooses his images in such a way as to paint a picture or to create a mood.

Canada has had a sufficient number of good descriptive writers to warrant calling attention to them as a separate group instead of including them under the heading of essayists. Some of these artists in description, such as Mrs. Jameson, Mrs. Moodie, Mrs. Traill, and F. P. Grove, have already been discussed. Others, such as Dr. MacMechan, Peter McArthur, and "Katherine Hale", will be considered in the fields in which the major portion of their work lies. Among those who deserve mention primarily for their descriptive work are Samuel T. Wood, W. H. Blake, and A. H. H. Heming.

Wood (1860-1917) was born on a backwoods farm in the Township of Wollaston, Ontario. When he was five years old, the family moved to Belleville. There he was educated at the public schools and at Belleville Business College. After a year in Peterborough, he went to Toronto in 1885, where he became a steamfitter by vocation and a park-meeting advocate of the Single Tax by avocation. He entered journalism, spent a year on an Ottawa newspaper, joined the staff of the Toronto *Globe* in 1891, and for more than a quarter of a century was an editor of that paper. He served as special correspondent in different parts of Canada and Newfoundland.

His writings include charmingly whimsical and humorous philosophical essays and nature articles. Because of his wide and accurate knowledge of nature and the winsomeness and grace of his style, his nature pieces rank among the best of their kind, as the student of Canadian literature will discover for himself by reading *Rambles of a Canadian Naturalist* (1916).

William Hume Blake (1861-1924) was born at Toronto, where he graduated in Arts from the University in

1882, and where, after being called to the Ontario bar in 1885, he practised the profession of law.

He translated into English in a manner worthy of high praise two of the most important books depicting the life of the French-Canadians of Quebec; Hémon's *Maria Chapdelaine* and Rivard's *Chez Nous*. His own *genre* pictures of French-Canadian life are excellently done. His humorous and colourful descriptive essays and sketches, as found in *Brown Waters* (1915) and *In a Fishing Country* (1922), are his best title to fame, and should place him permanently among the literary artists of Canada as a writer on Canadian nature and life in the open.

Arthur H. H. Heming (1870-........) was born at Paris, Ontario. An artist as well as a man of letters, he studied and taught at the Hamilton Art School, worked for the Dominion Illustrated, and was employed by Harper's to go as an artist to the remote regions of Canada. Some idea of his knowledge of the Canadian North and of his conscientiousness as a literary artist may be gathered from the statement that he made twenty-three voyages to the Northern woods and spent thirty-three years in collecting the information that constitutes the basis of one literary year in *The Drama of the Forest* (1921). And he is as careful in the revision of his work as he is in the gathering of his material. *The Drama of the Forest* was preceded by *Spirit Lake* (1907) and followed by *The Living Forest* (1925). All are written in a simple, direct, vivid style, and the illustrations, by the author himself, at least equal in artistic quality the material which they illustrate. By the mere power of his words alone, however, Heming is entitled to a place among those worthy to be remembered for the effective way in which they have described the Canadian scene.

CHAPTER 16

CANADIAN ESSAYISTS

Essays may be classified according to the nature of their material or according to the method of treating the material. On the former basis, essays are scientific, philosophical or reflective, historical, critical, editorial, descriptive, and personal, and the character sketch may be regarded as an essay. The classification according to method is the more suggestive one for the purposes of literary appreciation. On this basis, essays may be classified as formal and informal. The formal essay is logically planned and developed, and more naturally belongs to the literature of knowledge, as witness many magazine articles. The informal essay is the result not of logical treatment but of the play of personality or of temperamental association of ideas, or of both in combination. It is obvious, therefore, that for essays belonging to the literature of power we naturally turn to the informal essay.

In this type of literature two other characteristics are usually associated with the informality of structure. These are the use of personal experience, even of the first personal pronoun in reporting it, and the intimately conversational familiarity of the style. Because all three characteristics are likely to be found together in any essay of the type, the adjectives informal, personal, and familiar are used interchangeably to describe this form of literature. That they are so used should not be allowed to obscure for us the fact that they stand for different things, — for order of presentation, for source of material, and for manner of expression. Two other qualities commonly found in the informal essay, geniality and humour, are the result of the personal element. Not every person can please others while talking or writing about his own experience and using the first personal pronoun in the reporting of it. Such a person will seem egotistical unless he be gifted with a genial and humorous temperament. Essays that are pleasingly personal, therefore, are very likely to be delightfully genial and humorous in tone. Before turning to our major consideration in this discussion, Canada's contribution to the more literary type of essay, it may be well to mention the more important of the formal essayists of Canada.

Among the writers of editorial and critical material in the academic manner are J. Cappon, W. J. Alexander, M. Hutton, Bliss Carman, Pelham Edgar, and A. MacMechan, of whom the last two, as well as R. P. Baker, J. D. Logan, Lorne Pierce, A. MacMurchy, and T. G. Marquis, have written historical and critical works that cover the whole field of Canadian literature. Sir Andrew MacPhail writes with the logic of the formal essayist, but the easy familiarity of his style approaches that of the informal essayists of Canada, of whom the more noteworthy not considered duly under other types of literature are Sir William Osler, Thomas O'Hagan, Archibald MacMechan, "Janey Canuck", Stephen Leacock, and William Arthur Deacon.

Sir William Osler (1849-1919), son of a clergyman of English birth, was born at Bond Head, Ontario. In his veins flowed Cornish and Spanish blood. His education at Trinity College School, at Trinity College, University of Toronto, and at McGill University, Montreal, from which he graduated in Medicine in 1872, was supplemented by two years of professional study in London, Berlin, and Vienna. He taught medicine at McGill University from 1874 to 1884, at the University of Pennsylvania from 1884 to 1889, at Johns Hopkins University from 1889 to 1905, and at Oxford University from 1905 to 1919. In 1911 he was honoured with a baronetcy, and in the last year of his life with the presidency of the British Classical Association.

Notwithstanding his lifelong zeal for medical science and its application to the relief of human suffering, he found time for the pursuits of the scholar and the man of letters. Even his technical medical writings have a literary quality. His addresses to those directly interested in the study, teaching, and practice of medicine, and his biographical essays on great men in the medical profession, have a general appeal as literature and bear eloquent testimony in both style and content, not only that, as he says, Sir Thomas Browne was his "lifelong mentor" and the *Religio Medici* unsurpassed by any

[129]

other book in its influence on his life, but also that he was a keenly appreciative student of the Bible, of ancient science and philosophy, and of European, English, and American literary classics. The annals of Canada afford no finer example than Sir William Osler of the enrichment of life that comes from supplementing technical knowledge by a knowledge of the humanities.

Thomas O'Hagan (1855-........) was born near Toronto, the son of parents who were both natives of County Kerry, Ireland. During his infancy the family moved into the primeval wilds of Bruce County, so that Thomas experienced at first hand the conditions of pioneer life, and learned from his neighbours the Irish and the Highland Scottish forms of Gaelic. He was so capable a student that at the age of fifteen, having had such educational opportunities as could be provided in a country school taught by Irish and Scottish instructors of the old style, he was granted a second-class teacher's certificate. He spent four years at Saint Michael's College, Toronto, and won prizes in history, Latin, Greek, and English. Later he attended Ottawa University, from which he graduated in Arts in 1882, with honours in Latin, French, German, and English. He taught for a number of years and was principal of several High schools in Ontario. Always a student, he obtained the degree of Doctor of Philosophy from Syracuse University in 1889. He has studied also at Cornell and Chicago universities and the University of Wisconsin in the United States and at Louvain, Grenoble, and Bonn universities in Europe. He speaks four modern languages fluently and has some acquaintance with six other tongues. In recognition of his broad and deep scholarship, he has been the recipient of several honorary degrees. He has tried journalism as well as teaching, but for a number of years he has spent his time in travelling, lecturing, and writing.

O'Hagan has been publishing poetry for more than forty years and has appealed to the hearts of many with his simple, sincere, and melodious verse on a variety of subjects. His Celtic imagination and his broad human interests, enriched by wide reading and travel, fit him eminently for writing the literary essay, and probably his most distinctive work is in this form, volumes of which have been appearing for nearly thirty years. Of special interest to students of Canadian literature are *Canadian Essays* (1901) and *Intimacies in Canadian Life and Letters* (1927).

Archibald McKellar MacMechan (1862-........), was born at Berlin (now Kitchener), Ontario. He was educated at Picton Union School, at Hamilton Collegiate Institute, at the University of Toronto, from which he graduated with honours in modern languages in 1884, and, after teaching modern languages at Galt Collegiate Institute from 1885 to 1886, at Johns Hopkins University, from which he obtained the degree of Doctor of Philosophy in 1889. Since then he has been Professor of English Language and Literature at Dalhousie University, Halifax, Nova Scotia. He takes a keen interest in the history and literature of Canada in general and of Nova Scotia in particular, and has most

[131]

acceptably discharged the duties of President of the Nova Scotia Branch of the Canadian Authors' Association.

His writing has covered a wide range of material in a variety of literary forms. No scholar can fail to appreciate the decided literary charm of his critical, editorial, and historical work. His *Sagas of the Sea* (1924), and *Old Province Tales* (1924), annals of Nova Scotia based on fact, show a fine sense for narrative values. The soundness of his critical judgments and his felicitous expression of them are shown in his contributions, extending over more than twenty years, to the Montreal *Standard* under the pen name "The Dean", and in his book on Canadian literature. His purely creative writing includes two chap-books of well-written verse ranging from ballads to sonnets, and one large volume (*The Book of Ultima Thule* (1927)) of some of the finest local-colour writing in Canadian literature, and two volumes of literary essays. These last, with their delicate fancy, beautiful imagery, apt figures of speech, and lyric tone and structure, probably constitute his greatest contribution to Canadian literature and certainly rank him as a master of the literary essay in Canada.

"Janey Canuck", who in real life is Mrs. Emily Gowan (Ferguson) Murphy (1868-........), was born at Cookstown, Ontario, and was educated at Bishop Strachan School, Toronto. She is greatly interested in social welfare, as is indicated by the fact that she was a director of the Big Sisters Association from 1923 to 1925 and by her successful and helpful performance of her present duties as police magistrate in Edmonton, Alberta.

She has written colourful fiction, but her most notable work is in the field of the essay. Since 1910 she has been publishing collections of essays in book form. Her style is well suited to representation of the Middle West in the essay medium, and the first four volumes are of special interest in their material in that they are a study of the drug traffic.

William Arthur Deacon, a lawyer and the son of a lawyer, graduated from the University of Manitoba in 1918. He has had a variety of experience — as clerk, salesman, lawyer, and critic. His supreme interest is in books, and he has contributed to the book-review sections of the *New York Times* and the *New York Evening Post* and has acted as Canadian correspondent of the *Saturday Review of Literature* (New York). His articles have appeared not only in the best Canadian magazines but also in the *Christian Science Monitor* and the *American Mercury*. In May, 1922, he became literary editor of Toronto *Saturday Night,* and for practically six years made "The Book Shelf" a critical section that has never been surpassed, if indeed it has ever been equalled, in the literary history of Canada. After severing his connection with *Saturday Night,* he began to syndicate articles as a free-lance writer, and on the death of Fred Jacob (1928), became editor of the Saturday Book Page of the Toronto *Mail and Empire.*

[133]

Besides his biographical book on Peter McArthur, he has published *Pens and Pirates* (1923), *Poteen* (1926), and *The Four Jameses* (1927). Of these, *Poteen* best reveals his quality as an essayist. His wide experience of life and books stands him in good stead in the essay form, and no other familiar essayist of Canada can wield so piquant and trenchant a pen. Moreover, there is every reason to believe that his future work in this form will surpass his present achievement, if not in quality at least in quantity.

CHAPTER 17

CANADIAN HUMORISTS

Man has been defined as the animal who laughs. Whether or not man is unique among animals in his capacity for laughter, it is certain that he must laugh or go mad. So essential is laughter to man's well-being that he not only looks for the humorous in actual life but also creates literary forms of humour for his delectation. This attention to the comic in life and in literature justifies us in considering, under the special heading of Canadian humorists, writers that might have been discussed in connection with various types of literature, such as the essay, the short story, and the novel, for humour does not confine itself to any particular literary form.

Before taking up individual Canadian humorists, it may be well to consider in a simple and practical way the nature of the comic, on the subject of which there has been much philosophical discussion. For the purposes of practical appreciation of humour, it is sufficient to say that most humorous devices arouse in the reader or observer a feeling of superiority or a sense of incongruity, separately or in combination. Under conditions that do not arouse a feeling of deep sympathy or a strong fear of possible injury, it may be amusing to us to see a person slip on a piece of banana peel. We may laugh because the person, up to the moment of his fall, was in circumstances practically similar to our own but now is in a position of relative inferiority to us. There may also be an element of amusing incongruity between his state before the fall and that after, and the better dressed he is and the more dignified his habitual bearing, the greater this element of incongruity will be. The incongruous plays a very pronounced part in humorous writing, as witness the abundant use of dialect, misspelled words, verbal nonsense, odd figures of speech, exaggeration, parody, burlesque, and unexpected situations.

It is important not only to recognize the chief sources of humorous effects, but also to distinguish between high and low comedy. A very common error is the assumption that low comedy is necessarily cheap, vulgar, or even coarse. It may be all three, or it may be very clean and wholesome. Rightly understood, the term *low comedy* means that the humorous appeal is immediate and spontaneous. Such is the case, for example, when an intruder hides under a table on hearing the approach of someone, and does not get his hand completely under the table, so that the visitor accidentally steps on the hand and remains standing on it. High comedy, on the other hand, involves a process of intellectual activity, such as the making of a comparison or a contrast, before the comic element in the situation can be grasped.

[136]

The scenes between Beatrice and Benedick in Shakespeare's *Much Ado about Nothing,* after each has been privately told that the other is desperately in love with her or him respectively, are rich in high-comedy values. Low comedy results in instantaneous, unreflective laughter, high comedy in what George Meredith very aptly terms "thoughtful laughter". Humorous writings may rise to the level of literature by supplementing the low-comedy material with a sufficient amount of high-comedy material.

In this discussion of Canadian humorists it will not be possible to consider all Canadian writers who have written entertaining humour. It will be necessary to restrict our attention to those writers since Haliburton who may have written humorous material worthy to be ranked as literature in sufficient quantity to entitle them to a permanent record in the history of Canadian literature. Drummond will be the subject of a later study. E. W. Thomson will be discussed among the short-story writers, though he has some claim to be considered here, along with De Mille, Lanigan, Sara Jeanette Duncan, McArthur, and Leacock.

James De Mille (1833-80) was born at St. John, New Brunswick, of Loyalist ancestry on both his father's and his mother's side. He received his preparatory education at the Saint John grammar school and at Horton Academy. After his Freshman year at Acadia University, he and his brother made a visit to Europe, which included a walking tour in England and Scotland and travel through France and Italy, returning by way of the Alps. In 1852 he entered Brown

University, from which he received the degree of Master of Arts in 1854. After a year with friends in Cincinnati, he entered the book-selling business in Saint John, but found it financially unprofitable. Appointed Professor of Classics at Acadia University in 1860, he spent a year in preparation before beginning his work. In 1864 he was called to the chair of History and Rhetoric at Dalhousie University, which he filled from the time he left Acadia until his death. He had a good command of Latin, Greek, Hebrew, and half a dozen modern languages, and a working knowledge of Arabic and Sanskrit. He declined the position of Superintendent of Education for Nova Scotia, but probably would have accepted the chair of Rhetoric at Harvard University, had he not died while President Eliot was considering the matter of inviting him to take that position.

De Mille's tour of Europe greatly stimulated, if it did not produce, his desire to write, for he drew a great deal of his literary material from Italy, laid the scene of part or the whole of the action of many of his novels in that country, and began to write for magazines soon after the end of the tour. His fiction is of two classes, adult and juvenile, and is amazingly vast in amount in consideration of the fact that it was written in the spare time of a busy university professor. His large output of fiction for adults includes books such as one finds in Sunday-school libraries; sensational novels in the manners of Eugène Sue, Charles Reade, Wilkie Collins, and Jules Verne; comic novels of adventure, reminiscent of the literature of roguery in general and of Haliburton's *Slick* series in particular; an historical novel. His juvenile fiction includes the sprightly *B. O. W. C.* (Brethren of the White Cross) *Series,* six books suggested by his experiences at Acadia, the settings of which touch various parts of the Maritime Provinces and their coastal waters, and five of which have been published in the *American Boys' Series;* the noticeably inferior *Young Dodge Club Series,* suggested by his tour of Italy. In all of his fiction he stresses action and situation. Consequently there is much of caricature, farce, and melodrama, and at best only mild plausibility. He wrote to please not his artistic sense but public taste, and so fell short of greatness but attained wide popularity. His real personality is revealed in his mystic posthumously published poem *Behind the Veil* rather than in his prose fiction.

His work is so little Canadian in material that he was generally regarded as an American author. His novels of Rome in the time of the early Christians may have inspired *Ben Hur* and *Quo Vadis.* His chief literary influence is in the field of humour, and it is the humorous element in his work that constitutes his best chance of being remembered. Whether it is a matter of coincidence or of causal connection, "Mark Twain's" *The Innocents Abroad* was published a few months after De Mille's best comic novel of adventure, *The Dodge Club* (1869). That De Mille had a formative influence on American humour in general can hardly be doubted.

George Thomas Lanigan (1845-86), was born at Three Rivers in what is now the Province of Quebec. As a boy

[139]

he showed capacity as a linguist. He entered the field of journalism, founded what is now the Montreal *Star,* and acted as Canadian correspondent of a number of outstanding newspapers in the United States. He later moved to the United States. His first position there was on a St. Louis paper, of which, after one day as a reporter, he was made city editor as a result of the exceptional brilliance of a single piece of reportorial work. Interested in municipal and social problems, he roused a storm of wrath against himself and the newspaper by his criticism of influential cit-izens, and for the sake of his employers thought it best to resign. He spent some time as editor of one of the leading journals of Chicago, and then moved to New York, where he was for nine years on the staff of the *World* as an editorial writer and displayed some ability as a literary critic.

Lanigan wrote serious articles in good prose. His claim to remembrance, however, depends on his humour, and that largely because of the cleverness with which he cast his humorous material in two recognized literary forms, the ballad and the prose fable, examples of each of which have appeared in anthologies of American humour. The fables, printed first in the *World,* were later published in book form. In these he showed his keen and shrewd observation and understanding of the people and events of his time, and his capacity for satirizing human foibles in a clear, crisp, and pungent style.

Sara Jeanette Duncan (1862-1922), was born at Brant-ford, Ontario, and was educated at the Collegiate Institute there and at the Normal School, Toronto. Her native good taste was intensified by the classical quality of her education. After teaching for a time, she became the first Canadian-born woman journalist, and as such contributed material to the Toronto *Globe* (signing herself "Garth Grafton") and acted as correspondent for a number of papers in the United States and in Canada. She married Everard C. Cotes, of the Indian Museum, and in 1891 left Canada for Calcutta, India. She spent the greater part of her married life in India, but was in England at the time of her death.

Her first novel, *A Social Departure* (1890), revealed her literary skill not only in description and narration but also in brilliant humour, ranging from gentle whimsicality to caustic satire. The fame thus acquired was well sustained by a number of other novels published during the next decade and a half. Her native intellectual qualities, her knowledge of literature, her experience as a traveller, and her cosmopolitan outlook, eminently fitted her for writing humour of the high-comedy type, and in this respect she has never been surpassed by any Canadian humorist, if indeed she has ever been equalled.

Peter McArthur (1866-1924), born of Scottish parentage at Ekfrid, Ontario, was educated at the local public school, at Strathroy Collegiate Institute, and at University College, Toronto. After a short period of public-school teaching, he joined the staff of the Toronto *Mail and Empire* in 1889. In 1890 he went to New York. In 1895 he became assistant-editor, and later editor-in-chief and art manager, of *Truth*. From 1902 to 1904 he lived in London, England. In 1908, after four more years in New York as one of a firm of commercial publishers, he retired to his old home on the farm.

He wrote verse as well as prose. His reflective lyrics, chiefly sonnets on dreams, unfulfilled aspirations, and high moral endeavour, are sometimes deficient in rhythm and verbal music and too abstract in diction. Noticeably better are his poems of seasons and seasonal events and occupations, and his sprightly, humorous *vers de société*. It is as a humorous recorder of the events of life on the farm that he will live in Canadian literature. In this field he is unrivalled, as a reading of *In Pastures Green* (1915), *The Red Cow and her Friends* (1919), or any of the posthumously published volumes of his prose clearly shows.

Stephen Butler Leacock (1869-........), born at Swanmoor, Hampshire, England, came with his parents to a farm near Lake Simcoe, Ontario, in 1876. In 1887, on the completion of his course at Upper Canada College, Toronto, he entered the University of Toronto, from which he graduated in 1891. From that time until 1899 he was on the staff of Upper Canada College. The next four years he spent in graduate study for the degree of Doctor of Philosophy at the University of Chicago. Since then he has been on the faculty of McGill University. In 1917-8, under the auspices of the Cecil Rhodes Trust, he made a tour of the Empire, giving lectures on Imperial Organization.

His serious writing on serious subjects — political science, economics, biography, and history — belongs to the literature of knowledge, but some passages of biographical and historical narrative have literary style. His reputation as a man of letters depends on the best of the various prose writings that exemplify his partly or wholly humorous treatment of more or less serious subjects. To secure his comic effects he employs almost every device available to the humorist: sheer verbal nonsense, punning and word-play, sarcasm, irony, satire, exaggeration, caricature, farce, and burlesque. Though the results of these devices are not always equally satisfactory from the artistic point of view, nevertheless the quantity of his prose that attains to the quality of humorous literature makes him the greatest Canadian humorist since Haliburton.

CHAPTER 18

THE CANADIAN SHORT STORY

Not every story that is short is a short story in the technical sense. Short narratives are as old as the childhood of the race, but the short story proper, consciously written as such, is yet in the first century of its history. Short narratives cast in the typical short-story form by accident occur, of course, down through the ages, but the writing of the short story according to a consciously conceived technique seems to have been begun about 1835 simultaneously in France and the United States, in the latter country by Edgar Allan Poe. The theory of the short story set forth by Poe, except for his over-emphasis on atmosphere, is, with minor modifications, the theory of the typical short story of today.

The short story must produce singleness of effect. It does so by developing a unified plot to a climax. The typical short story builds its plot by weaving together two lines of action, and the vital part of the plot is the part between the point at which the two lines of action first come together and the point at which the united and unified lines

[144]

of action reach a climax. A good illustration is Will E.
Ingersoll's *The Man who Slept till Noon.* In this story,
a middle-aged man and a relatively young woman make a
common-sense match, he because he needs a housekeeper, she
because she wants a home. They live not unhappily together,
the wife becoming old rather too rapidly, till a young man is
hired to work on the farm owned by the couple. Youth
calls to youth in the young man and the young woman, and
as a result the woman becomes so attractive that her husband
falls desperately in love with her. The wife responds, and
they live much more happily because of the temporary
sojourn of the hired man in their midst.

In this story, the first line of action is the life of the
husband and wife before the arrival of the hired man.
The second line of action is the effect of the hired man
upon the wife. Neither of these would make a good story
alone, but the unification of the two lines of action makes
a very appealing story because of the change that is brought
about in the first line of action, the relationship between
husband and wife. The typical short-story plot thus has
two lines of action because only in exceptional circumstances
will one line of action brought to a climax make an effective story and because the scope of the short story will not
permit of handling more than two lines of action. If the
material be such that unity of time and place as well as of
action can be observed, so much the better.

From this it is evident that the term *short story* as
sometimes used, by Knister for example, includes many

short narratives that are not short stories in the technical sense. In order to be as technically accurate as possible in our use of terms, we may use for all short narratives the comprehensive term *tales*. All short stories are tales, but only such tales are short stories as conform to the typical short-story technique. Whether this ought to be so or whether it will remain so, the point is that at present it is so. Since, however, the term *short story* has been applied in Canadian literature to many tales that are not short stories proper, the student of Canadian short fiction is afforded the opportunity of increasing his aesthetic pleasure and of developing his power of literary discrimination by deciding for himself whether any particular piece of short fiction is or is not a typical short story.

Several Canadian writers of tales, such as Parker, Stringer, and L. M. Montgomery, have been considered among the novelists. W. A. Fraser was discussed among the writers of animal stories, and the tales of C. G. D. Roberts and of D. C. Scott will be noticed in connection with their work as a whole. Besides these, there have been scores of Canadian authors of short fiction of varying degrees of excellence. Obviously, these cannot all be taken up here, or even mentioned by name. The most that can be done is to discuss some of the more significant whose work in this field is either completed or, if still in progress, is suggestive because of its material or its method. Such are E. W. Thomson, W. McLennan, Mrs. Rogers, Norman Duncan, and F. W. Wallace.

[146]

Edward William Thomson (1849-1924), son of a banker and litterateur descended from a Lowland Scottish Loyalist, was born near Toronto, and was educated at the public schools of Caledonia and Brantford, Ontario, and at Trinity College Grammar School, Weston, Ontario. He enlisted in the United States Army before he reached the age of sixteen, and participated in the last year of the Civil War. He returned to Canada, joined the Queen's Rifles of Toronto, and helped to suppress the Fenians. Subsequently he practised the profession of civil engineering until 1878. From 1879 to 1881 he was chief editorial writer of the Toronto *Globe*. For the next ten years he was a literary editor of the *Youth's Companion,* Boston, and a writer of short stories. Then he removed to Ottawa and devoted himself to general literary work. After his wife's death in 1921 he returned to Boston to spend his last days near his only grandson.

Though he has received recognition in England and the United States as well as in Canada for inspirational verse and political prose inbreathed with noble patriotism, lofty idealism, broad human sympathy, and buoyant faith in mankind, his short stories, including excellent stories for boys, constitute his chief literary distinction. His skill in creating types, British and French, in revealing the comic and the tragic in ordinary life, in vivid portrayal of setting and local colour, and in constructing plots strong in suspense and in moral heroism in action, rank him among the few Canadian masters of the short story.

[147]

William McLennan (1856-1904), born in Montreal, was educated at the High School there and at McGill University, from which he graduated in Law, with distinction, in 1880. In addition to practising law, he filled useful and honourable positions in his native city. Two years of travel in Europe for his health preceded his death in Vallambrosa, Italy.

Though he has written commendable verse and has translated French-Canadian folk-songs, his literary reputation depends upon his prose. His *Spanish John* (1898) shows the influence of picaresque fiction, especially as written by Lever and burlesqued by Thackeray, and is reminiscent of Stevenson's *Kidnapped* in its use for fictional purposes of Jacobite material, chiefly after Culloden. *The Span of Life* (1899), in which he collaborated with Jean McIlwraith, passes quickly from Jacobite interest to adventures in what is now Canada during the last years of rivalry between the English and French. Skill in bringing the characters together is somewhat offset by failure to develop adequately what promised to be great situations. McLennan's prose tales constitute his most distinctive work, and of these, his sympathetic narratives of French-Canadian life, with their humour, pathos, and local colour, are of most significance in the history of Canadian literature. They challenge comparison with similar tales by Duncan Campbell Scott and with Drummond's *habitant* verse.

Mrs. Grace Dean (McLeod) Rogers (1865-........), a native of Nova Scotia, was educated at Dalhousie University,

Halifax. Her contribution to Canadian short fiction is of significance not merely because she knows how to tell a good story but also because her tales are based on legends of Nova Scotia, especially those concerned with the French Acadians. *Stories of the Land of Evangeline* was first published in 1891. A new edition in 1923 omits some of the stories found in the first edition and includes some new ones. The new edition has called forth numerous favourable reviews in the years since its publication.

Norman Duncan (1871-1916), born at Brantford, Ontario, spent his boyhood in various Canadian towns. He attended the University of Toronto from 1891 to 1895, and participated eagerly in literary activity. After leaving the University he spent two years on the staff of the *Auburn Bulletin* and four years on the staff of the *New York Evening Post*. In 1900, as correspondent of *McClure's Magazine,* he spent the first of his three summers in Newfoundland, which, supplemented by a summer on the Labrador coast, furnished him with important material for fiction. From 1901 to 1906 he was at Washington and Jefferson College, for one year as assistant to the Professor of English, and for four years as Professor of Rhetoric. He was correspondent for *Harper's Magazine* in Palestine, Arabia, and Egypt in 1907 and 1908, and in Australia, New Guinea, the Dutch East Indies, and the Malay States in 1912 and 1913. Between these two periods of travel he was for two years Adjunct Professor of English Literature at the University of Kansas. Though he passed most of his adult life in the United States, he never took out citizenship papers there, and after his death in New York, his body was brought to the place of his birth for burial.

His travel sketches, especially the later ones, are reminiscent of Dickens's *Pickwick Papers*. His fiction, with its use and exaggeration of the bizarre and grotesque in setting, situation, and character, and with its sentiment, notably in Christmas stories and in his treatment of children and mentally weak adults, is decidedly Dickensian. In conformity with the taste of his period and probably with his own genius, he employs chiefly the shorter forms of narrative, and goes beyond his master in dialect, local colour, and atmosphere, as exemplified in his stories of the Syrian quarter in New York, of the Florida Keys, of the lumber camps of northern Minnesota, and, his supreme achievement, of the fishing villages of Newfoundland and the Labrador Coast.

Frederick William Wallace (1886-........) was born at Ibrox, Glasgow, Scotland, the son of a Scottish father and an English mother. He was educated at private school, at the Glasgow public schools, and at Allan Glen's School, Glasgow. He visited Canada in 1895. In 1902 he took a position with the Allan Line at Glasgow. In 1904 he came to Canada with his parents, and the family settled at Hudson, Quebec. He had a variety of employment up till 1908, when he became a free-lance writer and illustrator, specializing in literature of the sea. He sailed from American and Canadian ports in various classes of ships. In 1909 he became interested in the Canadian fisheries, and in order to make his study of the industry as thorough as possible, went as a fisherman to the various fishing banks of the North Atlantic. In 1910 he was for a time on the staff of the *Canadian Century*. He joined the Industrial and Educational Press in 1913, began the *Canadian Fisherman* in 1915, and took a leading part in organizing the Canadian Fisheries Association, the affairs of which he managed and directed till the beginning of 1922. While editor of the *Canadian Fisherman* he continued his work as a practical fisherman on board all kinds of fishing vessels in the Atlantic, the Great Lakes, and the Pacific. After some special naval service during the Great War, he was in 1917 put in charge of the technical side of the Fish Section, Canada Food Board, of which Section he was later made Superintendent. He also acted in an advisory capacity to the United States Government in the administration of the fishing industry. In 1922 he went to New York as editor of the *Fishing Gazette,* of which, now published at Boston, he is still editor. He has used his varied experience of the sea in writing thrilling tales, and has won for himself a distinctive place by novels and short stories of Canadian fishermen, as his novel *The Viking Blood* (1921), and collections of short fiction like *Shack Locker* (1916) amply attest.

CHAPTER 19

CANADIAN DRAMA

Drama is the most realistic form of literary art because in it actual people present by dialogue and action a picture of life on a stage that is usually made to imitate actuality as closely as possible. This most realistic of literary arts has been almost wholly neglected in Canada, a state of affairs that causes the student of Canadian literature to ask several questions. Does Canadian life lend itself to realistic treatment? Is Canadian life so complete in its actuality that we do not need, desire, or have time to spend upon, realistic literature of Canadian life? Does realistic treatment of Canadian life, especially in dramatic form, demand a measure of creative ability to which our men and women of letters, for some reason or combination of reasons, have not yet to any marked degree attained?

Each one of these questions must be answered, in some measure at least, in the affirmative. In the first place, Canadian life does not lend itself readily to realistic treatment because it has, generally speaking, been so uniformly happy. It is difficult to write great realistic literature about communities in which the vast majority of members are in a chronic state of well-being. Such literature is usually based on the struggle and suffering involved in overcoming great hardships. It is significant that most of our small amount of good realistic fiction is the story of the struggle of immigrants or of others who have had to fight the unwilling forces of nature for the necessities of life. Then, too, Canadians have for the most part experienced actual Canadian life richly and fully enough not to need realistic imitations of Canadian life. Again, realistic treatment of life does demand a higher level of creative ability than does romantic literature, as may be inferred from the fact that so vast a majority of Canadian novels are romantic. And the drama is a decidedly more difficult form than the novel, so that realistic drama makes unusually heavy demands on the creative ability of the literary artist. Moreover, drama depends for its success on an immediate public gathered together in a theatre. No matter how earnestly a playwright may strive to write realistic drama, it will be of no avail unless he can find a sufficiently large audience to appreciate his efforts, and the fact of the matter seems to be that Canadian taste is far more for the romantic than for the realistic. Thus for a variety of reasons Canadian literature is poor in drama and especially so in realistic drama of Canadian life.

The most significant of the few full-length plays that we have in Canadian literature are romantic dramas in poetic form, most of them directly imitative of Shakespeare. The first notable drama written in Canada in imitation of Shakespeare was *Saul* (1857), by Charles Heavysege (1816-76), an English immigrant to Canada. This drama was highly praised by men of letters at the time, but it had no influence on Canadian dramatic literature. Mair's *Tecumseh* (1886), imitative of Shakespeare's chronicle plays even to the extent of introducing realistic and occasionally humorous touches by means of the less dignified characters in the play, was never intended for the stage. It is of interest because it makes some use of the Canadian scene during the war of 1812. William Wilfred Campbell avowedly modelled the contents of his *Poetical Tragedies* (1908) on the work of Shakespeare because he regarded him as the supreme dramatist of the world. Of these tragedies only *Daulac* is set in Canada, and that only in part.

Interesting as are these attempts to transplant the Shakespeare tradition in Canadian soil, one may question the appropriateness of the poetic form of drama as a literary medium for the expression of Canadian life. Moreover, these writers imitated Shakespeare's methods not only when they were good but also when they were unsound according to modern principles of dramatic technique. For example, not content with writing their drama in the conventional blank verse and in the conventional five-act form, they divided their acts into a number of scenes, whereas, according to the best modern stagecraft, there should be only one scene to an act. Whether or not the imitators of Shakespeare were artistically right, they failed to establish a Canadian school of poetic drama in the Shakespearean tradition.

Not all full-length poetic drama by Canadian authors is wholly on the Shakespearean model. Arthur Stringer's poems in dramatic form are like Shakespeare's only in that they are written in blank verse, are dramatic only in the sense that they are presented by dialogue and action, and are Canadian only in that the author spent part of his life in Canada, the themes being classical. Robert Norwood's powerful poetical dramas on Biblical themes, *The Witch of Endor* (1916) and *The Man of Kerioth* (1919), both tragedies, depart freely from the mature Shakespearean pattern in the abundant use of rhyme with a variety of rhyme schemes and of metres other than iambic pentameter. Norwood has not yet written a drama on a Canadian theme.

Full-length plays in prose by Canadian authors are more rare than poetic dramas, and of these, *The God of Gods* (printed in 1927), by Carroll Aikins, and *Marsh Hay* (printed in 1923), by Merrill Denison,, are the only two of any significance that are on Canadian subjects. The influence of Aikins and Denison on the development of Canadian drama may best be indicated in a survey of the one-act play, a form the history of which is closely associated with the Little Theatre movement.

This movement had its origin in the Free Theatre founded in Paris in 1837 by André Antoine. He loved artistic drama and hated the commercial theatre because it sacrificed art for financial returns. He organized a group of kindred spirits, who were not bound by the traditions of producers and actors, and who were not interested in big profits. They devised new kinds of setting and new ways of producing plays, and put on new sorts of plays by new authors. They developed "naturalism" in style, and because their theatre was small, there was an artistically helpful intimacy between actors and audience.

The Little Theatres continued the work of the Free Theatre. They stand particularly for experimentation, non-commercialism, and the kind of intimacy that gives the audience a share in making the play effective. This intimacy can best be obtained in a small theatre. Before the Great War, Little Theatres had spread pretty well to the centres of culture in Europe, and in some the actors put on their own plays. The movement reached the United States in 1911-2, and by 1917 there were at least fifty in that country. Dozens have disappeared, but there are still some very important ones, and the movement has exerted a beneficial influence on drama. The Little Theatres have made possible the presentation of types of plays that could not be presented in large theatres. They have encouraged amateur acting, and by making scenery less elaborate, have stimulated the audience to greater use of the imagination. They have encouraged new writers, especially natives. They have afforded a special opportunity for the one-act play.

In Canada the idea has been developed by City and University groups of actors. Vancouver, Edmonton, Winnipeg, and Montreal, among Canadian cities, and the universities of British Columbia, Alberta, and Toronto, have achieved distinction in this respect. The Montreal Branch of the Canadian Authors' Association published a volume of one-act plays in 1926, and already there are two volumes of *Canadian Plays from Hart House Theatre* (1926, 1927).

The name of Carroll Aikins is associated with the founding in 1920 of the Home Theatre, at Naramata, in the Okanagan Valley, British Columbia. This theatre aims particularly to foster the development of native drama. Every encouragement is given to Canadian talent, and Mr. Aikins looks forward to a time when Canadian authors will produce great plays, Canadian in material and in spirit.

The name of Merrill Denison is closely associated with Hart House Theatre, Toronto. In order not to misunderstand the tone of Denison's realism the reader needs to know that Denison's dramatic work is a two-fold protest: against the restriction of the dramatic field to the treatment of the romantic and the heroic in poetical form: against the unreal, sentimental, heroic, and romantic treatment of life in much of so-called "Western fiction". Because his realism is a protest against an existing condition in literature, it is more bitter than it would otherwise have been, just as Thackeray was more bitterly realistic by way of protest than he would have been if there had been nothing to protest against. Denison's dramatic work, with its studies of life in backwoods and rural Canadian communities, has encouraged the realistic treatment of Canadian life and the development of the one-act play.

[157]

The one-act play has been written for the most part in prose, the most notable exception being Marjorie Pickthall's excellent poetic drama, *The Wood Carver's Wife* (1920). Whatever may be the opinion as to the appropriateness of the poetic form of drama for tragedy, there can be no question as to the greater suitability of prose for comedy. Some notable comedies have been written in Canada in the one-act form and in prose. In addition to the anthologies of one-act plays previously mentioned, there have been volumes of plays in a single act by such writers as Fred Jacob (died 1928) and Mazo de la Roche and individual plays by poets like Duncan Campbell Scott and Marian Osborne. The fact that writers in other fields have turned their attention to the one-act play in prose is clear evidence that the form is attracting attention in a measure that promises well for its future.

There can be little doubt that the future of dramatic art in Canada depends on the success of the Little Theatres and the Community Playhouses. It also seems highly probable that the form that will receive the greatest impetus through the encouragement of these experimental theatres will be the one-act form. This form, like the modern short story, is well suited to the rapid tempo of modern life. One of the chief arguments against it is that it is difficult for an audience to adjust itself quickly enough to a series of entirely different dramatic themes in an evening's bill of one-act plays. This does not seem to be a very cogent objection when one considers the ease with which an audience adjusts itself to different types of musical compositions in an evening's entertainment or the still greater ease with which a vaudeville audience adjusts itself to a "variety show". Because of its concentration, its conformity with all the unities, and its skilful development of a single dramatic crisis, the well-written one-act play is a piece of consummate art, and it well may be one of the most important of future Canadian forms.

CHAPTER 20

EARLY POETS

The student of our literature cannot get a full appreciation of Canadian poetry without paying particular attention to imagery. This subject was discussed in a practical way in Chapter 15. There we saw the basic importance of imagery in descriptive prose. Good imagery is even more vitally essential to descriptive poetry, because the fact that the material has been put into verse form arouses greater aesthetic expectations on the part of the reader. In poetry other than descriptive, too, imagery is of the greatest artistic value, because it is through concrete language that the imagination is stimulated into activity, and the two outstanding means of concreteness are images and figures of speech. Figurative language is of great value to the poet because it may be used when literal images are impossible, as in the case of reflective poetry. Thought, being by nature abstract, can receive artistic expression only by being translated into the concrete, and this can be done only by the use of figures of speech, for there are no images that, taken as a group, form a mental picture of a thought, as there are images that, properly assembled, enable us to see in the mind's eye, a scene, an object, or a person. Other things being equal, the effectiveness of poetry depends on the concreteness of the poet's diction, that is, on his use of images and figures of speech.

We have noticed the poetry of Alline under Puritan literature, that of Stansbury and Odell under Loyalist literature, that of McLachlan under Scottish literature, that of Howe in our study of his life and work. Drummond will receive special consideration later. Other early Canadian poets worthy of comment here are Oliver Goldsmith, Thomas D'Arcy McGee, Charles Sangster, Charles Mair, Isabella Valancy Crawford, and George Frederick Cameron.

Oliver Goldsmith (1781-1861), grand-nephew of the English poet of the same name, was born at Annapolis, Nova Scotia, in the year in which his father, a Loyalist and ex-soldier of the American Revolution, settled there. His work as a poet implies that he received an education, and his appointment, after a period of clerkship, as Commissary General of Nova Scotia, suggests that the family attained to some social standing. He moved to England, and died at Liverpool.

His verse is strongly reminiscent of that of his English relative in its descriptive and sentimental material and in its predominating use of the heroic couplet, but it departs from the neo-classical norm in the use of octosyllabic couplets and anapaestic feet. His writings include passable metrical psalms, lyrics of mild sentiment, mock epic and comic poems, patriotic New Year's addresses in verse, and his masterpiece, *The Rising Village* (1825), the first poem of any length by

[161]

a native author to be published in both Great Britain and Canada. It is significant as the first poetic representation of the experiences by which the Loyalists triumphed over home-sickness and material obstacles and came to love and have faith in Canada, the land of their adoption.

Thomas D'Arcy McGee (1825-68), whose parents were both descended from Irish patriots and whose cultured mother was the daughter of a Dublin bookseller ruined by his participation in the Rebellion of 1798, was born at Carlingford, County Louth, Ireland. When he was eight years old, the family moved from the beautiful scenes of his birthplace to the historic town of Wexford, at a day-school in which he received his only formal education. Soon after moving to Wexford he lost his mother, to whom he was indebted for his religious temperament and for his love and knowledge of Irish folk-lore. At the age of seventeen, four years after his first display of his natural gift for oratory, he went to the United States. There he achieved such a reputation as a writer and public speaker that before he was twenty he returned to London as a correspondent for the Irish press. When the "Young Ireland" movement, which he had joined in 1846, failed in 1848, he escaped to the United States in the disguise of a priest. Although he established there between 1848 and 1853 two newspapers in the interest of the Irish cause, such were the attacks on him of the extreme Irish revolutionaries that in 1857 he moved to Lower Canada. To the bar of this province he was admitted in 1861. His career in its Parliament began with his election in 1858 as member for Montreal and culminated in his appointment as Minister of Agriculture in 1864. An active supporter of Confederation, he was elected to the first Dominion Parliament in 1867. A few months later, because of his opposition to the Fenian invasion, he was assassinated at the instigation of some members of the race to the cause of whose freedom he had devoted his life.

His versatility challenges comparison with that of Joseph Howe, but Howe's temperament may be described as essentially epic, McGee's as essentially lyric. In his verse, two intense social emotions, patriotism and loyalty to his Church, are fused with the more private emotions of friendship and domestic affection into a flaming passion for the freedom of Ireland. The adverse conditions that deferred his hope resulted in many poems exemplifying the heroism of leaders in similar causes in Irish and general history. The stirring, light, and evidently spontaneous rhythms, abounding in trochaic and trisyllabic feet, which he used to rouse and encourage his countrymen, became a permanent and somewhat monotonous characteristic of his verse. His style, occasionally reminiscent of Wordsworth, Coleridge, Longfellow, Goldsmith, and Burns, is most like that of Moore. His oratory and his historical and biographical prose, in which his style shows a development in ease, eloquence, and urban tone, are inspired largely by the same emotions as his verse. Significantly, however, from the Canadian point of view, in his later prose he looks to the future of Canada for the realization of his dream of civil and religious liberty in a unified nation. In the preface to his *Canadian Ballads* (1858) he also foresees an enduring Canadian national literature.

Charles Sangster (1822-93), son of a joiner in the British Navy and grandson on his father's side of a Scottish United Empire Loyalist who fought in the American Revolution, and on his mother's side of a Scottish settler in Ontario, was born at the Navy Yard, Point Frederick, Kingston, Ontario. At two years of age he lost his father. At fifteen, he left school in order to help his mother support the family. He was employed first in the manufacture of cartridges in the naval laboratory at Fort Henry during the troubles of 1837, and then in a subordinate position in the Ordnance Office, Kingston, for several years. Early a contributor of prose and verse to periodicals, including the *Literary Garland,* he turned his attention seriously to literary work when appointed editor of the Amherstburg *Courier* in 1849. The next year he resigned, returned to Kingston, and became proof reader on the *Whig.* He held this position until, at the age of forty-six, he entered the Civil Service at Ottawa, and while holding it also did some work for the Kingston *Daily News.* After taking his Civil Service position, he seems to have had no time for literary pursuits.

Sangster's birth, education, and life work made him Canadian in thought and feeling. In his poetry he caught the spirit of the nationalistic movement inaugurated by the *Literary Garland* to employ Canadian material. His verse,

[164]

though imitative, first of Byron and then of Longfellow, Tennyson, and Wordsworth, shows a genuine poetic appreciation of Canadian scenery, a gift for lyrics of love and patriotism, and some measure of skill in interpreting as well as describing nature. He is the first Canadian poet to make extensive use of Canadian subject matter.

Charles Mair (1838-1927), of Scottish and English ancestry, was born at Lanark, Ontario. He was educated at the village school there, at Perth Grammar School, and at Queen's University. In the spring of 1868 he gave up the medical course for which he had returned to Queen's and entered Government service at Ottawa, where he became one of the first five members of the "Canada First" party. His work associated him with the movement to acquire the Hudson's Bay Company lands for Canada, first as a clerk working on the records, and then as paymaster and press reporter of the party sent to build a road between Fort Garry (Winnipeg) and the Lake of the Woods. By his correspondence from the West to the Toronto *Globe* and the Montreal *Gazette,* filled as it was with Canadian national spirit, he corrected the politic misrepresentation of the Hudson's Bay Company, revealed the truth about the prairies, and so greatly stimulated settlement. Three months after his marriage at Winnipeg in 1869, the first Riel rebellion broke out. The rebels stole a trunk containing the wedding silver and precious manuscripts, imprisoned the couple, and sentenced him to death. He escaped, and later engaged in the fur trade, first at Portage la Prairie and then at Prince

[165]

Albert, until he moved to Windsor, Ontario, in 1883. During the second Riel rebellion he was quartermaster in the Governor-General's Body Guard. He helped found Kelowna, British Columbia, went with a Government party through the Mackenzie basin, and, in the service of the Immigration Department, sojourned in Winnipeg, Lethbridge, Coutts, and Fort Steele. He died at Victoria, British Columbia.

Mair's poetry has a sensuousness reminiscent of Keats. Much of his early work is inartistic because he had not mastered the principle of selection either in the presentation of descriptive details or in the development of a unified narrative. The later poems and the revisions of the earlier ones show a marked advance in artistic condensation. His poetic closet drama has already been discussed in the section on Canadian drama. The significance of his work in general is that it shows the literary value of Canadian material and emphasizes the necessity, without any weakening of the bonds of Empire, of a strong national consciousness as a basis for Canadian achievement.

Isabella Valancy Crawford (1850-87), daughter of a sensitive and refined gentlewoman and a scholarly physician, was born on Christmas day, in Dublin, Ireland, one of a large family. In 1857, the father, hoping to find greater economic prosperity in one of Britain's colonies, visited Australia to spy out the land. Recalled by sickness in his family, he returned to find that seven of his children had died of fever. In 1858, the family came to Canada. During the six years that they lived at Paisley, Ontario, two more

of the children died. The life at Paisley furnished Isabella
with ample opportunity for the observation of pioneer life.
Reduced to a state of semi-poverty, the remaining family
moved first to Lakefield and then to Peterborough. The
father died in 1875, the only remaining sister soon after,
and as the only brother was working in the wilds, Isabella
and her mother were the only two living together when
they moved to humble quarters in Toronto. There, Miss
Crawford, to support herself and her mother, wrote with
untiring zeal until she died suddenly of heart failure.

She early began to write both prose and verse. Her
work in the short story, though it attracted some notice,
is insignificant in comparison with her poetry. Her outstanding literary merits are formal excellence, verbal music,
philosophical insight, emotional intensity and range, and
dramatic imagination almost universal in scope. The last
two in particular give to her poetry variety, from the most
delicate lyric play of Celtic fancy to the elemental grandeur
of primitive epic. Her narrative poems, whether in blank
verse or in rhymed stanza, whether in dialect or in literary
language, describe settings with a Keats-like vividness, and
at times present dramatic situations, both serious and comic,
with Shakespearean effectiveness. Her lyrics include Shelley-
like interpretations of the spirit of personified natural
objects, and Browning-like dramatic lyrics presenting great
emotional moments in the lives of persons of many social

[167]

ranks, countries, and periods. Notwithstanding her broad sympathy, she was essentially Canadian in spirit. She has an unrivalled position as Canada's greatest female poet.

George Frederick Cameron (1854-85) was born of Scottish ancestry at New Glasgow, Nova Scotia, and received his preparatory education at the High School there. Three years after the removal of the family to Boston in 1869, he began his course at the Boston University of Law, on the completion of which he entered a law office. He devoted himself chiefly to literature, however, and contributed to various Boston papers. In 1882 he entered Queen's University, Kingston, Ontario, and the next year was prize poet. From March of that year until a few weeks before his death, he was editor of the Kingston *News*.

His lyrics on freedom, some of them written in his early teens, though they voice no philosophy of liberty, exemplify his theory that the true poet has "an utterance for his age", in their agonized, Shelley-like protest against injustice and tyranny. His lyrics on love, in which kind he ranks himself next to Sappho, are chiefly poignant expressions of the pain of the lover at the loss of his lady's love, sometimes with a Byronic imputation that women in general are inconstant. A similar emotional intensity characterizes most of his lyrics on other subjects. His own explanation of the note of sorrow and suffering is that his poetry had its origin in sorrow, that "sorrow, song, and life were at one altar lit". Like Shelley, a sufferer because of the effect upon his intense emotional temperament of man's inhumanity to man; like

[168]

him, he has the rare felicity and range of technique that give each kind of lyric material its most appropriate expression. Because of his excellence of form and his cosmopolitan sympathy with mankind, his poetry is not of Canada merely but of the world.

CHAPTER 21

C. G. D. ROBERTS
(1860-........)

Charles George Douglas Roberts has been called the Dean of Canadian Literature, a very appropriate title, not only because of his seniority among writers who belong to the national period of Canadian history, but also because of the diversity of his literary gifts as poet, historian, translator, novelist, and writer of short stories, especially of animal life. He is the most distinguished member of Canada's most distinguished literary family. Two brothers and a sister have published verse, one of these brothers has written many volumes of prose fiction, a son is one of the leaders of the mature younger poets, a young niece, daughter of the brother who has written verse and fiction, has recently begun to attract favourable attention by her verse, and Bliss Carman was a first cousin to the subject of our present study.

Charles G. D. Roberts, on his mother's side a distant cousin of Ralph Waldo Emerson, was born at Douglas, York County, New Brunswick, and spent the first fourteen years of his life at Westcock, at the mouth of the Tantramar River, in a region which he has made famous in his poetry. In 1876 he passed from the Fredericton Grammar School, where the head-master, George R. Parkin, had already awakened in him the love of literature, to the University of New Brunswick, from which he was graduated in 1879, with honours in Mental and Moral Science and Political Economy. For several years he taught in the grammar schools of New Brunswick. Then for a short time he edited the Toronto *Week*. From 1885 to 1895 he held a professorship at the University of King's College, then at Windsor, Nova Scotia, teaching various subjects, chiefly English literature. After resigning his professorship he made his home in New York, with frequent visits to Canada and Great Britain. Except for a brief tenure of an associate-editorship of the *Illustrated American,* he devoted himself entirely to literature until he enlisted as a trooper in the Legion of Frontiersmen in September, 1914. During his period of military service his family lived at Ottawa. After the Great War he lived in England till his return to Canada in 1925. Since then he has been honoured with the Lorne Pierce Medal of the Royal Society of Canada for his contribution to Canadian literature, and with the presidency of the Canadian Authors' Association.

Noticeable in the early works of Roberts are his poems on classic subjects after the manner of Keats. In his treatment of classic themes, the outstanding poetic success is the creation of imaginary landscapes. These he describes in imagery drawn not only from the reading of classical literature, but also from the observation of Canadian nature. From his classical material, therefore, he passes easily to

[171]

vivid description in which the imagery is drawn wholly from his accurate observation of Canadian nature. His descriptive poetry reaches its highest degree of excellence in the Canadian scenes represented in the sonnet sequence entitled *Songs of the Common Day* (1893). So great an artist would not limit his work to description. Another normal change takes place in *The Book of the Native* (1896); the treatment of nature becomes thoughtful rather than descriptive. Occasional poems have a moral turn after the manners of Longfellow and Wordsworth, and in general Roberts approaches nature with Emersonian mysticism. This mysticism, however, is modified by a comprehensive knowledge of modern science, so that the discoveries resulting from mystical meditation are never in conflict with ascertained fact. With fine balance Roberts speculates on cosmic processes and voices his philosophy in melodious verse.

After he removed to New York, Roberts wrote a few representations of city environment somewhat in the manner of his successful nature poetry. In the main, however, he changed from the poetry of nature to the poetry of man, or more strictly speaking, to the poetry of woman, for his verse now became predominantly erotic, sometimes with the delicate reserve of Rossetti at his best, sometimes with the emotional abandon of Swinburne and his master, Baudelaire. Since the Great War Roberts has turned once more to poetry that expresses the consolation and moral stimulus of nature and a remarkably well-balanced philosophic idealism.

[172]

In addition to his great achievement in poetry, Roberts has written two kinds of prose fiction; fiction with human characters and fiction with animal characters. In the former he has written both tales and novels. Because he has not the gift of genius in interpreting human character, he did not attain distinction in this kind of fiction, except where the setting gave him an opportunity to show his great skill in picturing nature. In his animal fiction he was free to characterize in accordance with his own standard of probability and to exercise to the full his consummate artistry in nature description. His sympathetic interpretation of animal life has won for him the title of "Poet Laureate of the Animal World." Even those who contend that he has humanized his animals too much must succumb to the poetic charm with which he has reproduced the *habitat* of his animal heroes, for whatever his literary medium, he excels in description of Canadian nature.

No better way of appreciating Roberts's descriptive powers can be suggested than that of choosing illustrative examples from his poems picturing various aspects of the different seasons of the Canadian year. Winter fields are described thus:

"Winds here, and sleet, and frost that bites like steel.
The low bleak hill rounds under the low sky.
Naked of flock and fold the fallows lie,
Thin streaked with meagre drift. The gusts reveal
By fits the dim grey snakes of fence, that steal

[173]

Through the white dusk. The hill-foot poplars sigh,
While storm and death with winter trample by,
And the iron fields ring sharp, and blind lights reel."

Contrast this with the following description of the inside of an old barn:

"Tons upon tons the brown-green fragrant hay
O'erbrims the mows beyond the time-warped eaves,
Up to the rafters where the spider weaves,
Though few flies wander his secluded way.
Through a high chink one lonely golden ray,
Wherein the dust is dancing, slants unstirred.
In the dry hush some rustlings light are heard,
Of winter-hidden mice at furtive play."

And consider next his pictorial representation of that exquisite natural phenomenon, the silver thaw:

"The silvered saplings, bending,
Flashed in a rain of gems.
The statelier trees, attending,
Blazed in their diadems.
White fire and amethyst
All common things had kissed,
And chrysolites and sapphires
Adorned the bramble-stems.

In crystalline confusion
All beauty came to birth."

[174]

In describing the Canadian spring, Roberts is equally effective whether he takes you in quest of the arbutus or of brook trout:

"For days the drench of noiseless rains,
Then sunshine on the vacant plains,
And April with her blind desire
A vagrant in my veins!

* * * * *

At length within a leafy nest,
Where spring's persuasions pleaded best,
I found a pale, reluctant flower,
The purpose of my quest."

* * * * *

"The airs that blew from the brink of day
Were fresh and wet with the breath of May.
I heard the babble of brown brooks falling
And golden-wings in the woodside calling.

* * * * *

Big drops hung from the sparkling eaves;
And through the screen of the thin young leaves
A glint of ripples, a whirl of foam,
Lured and beckoned me out from home.

* * * * *

Lurked in their watery lairs the trout
But, silver and scarlet, I lured them out.

I whipped the red pools under the beeches;
I whipped the yellow and dancing reaches.
The purple eddy, smooth like oil,
And the tail of the rapid yielded spoil."

From many passages descriptive of summer scenes one may choose parts of "The Mowing" and "An August Wood Road":

"This is the voice of high midsummer's heat.
The rasping vibrant clamour soars and shrills
O'er all the meadowy range of shadeless hills . . . . .
The crying knives glide on; the green swath lies.
And all noon long the sun, with chemic ray,
Seals up each cordial essence in its cell . . . . . "

* * * * *

"All day long till day is done
Sleeps in murmuring solitude
The worn old road that threads the wood.
In its deep cup — grassy cool —
Sleeps the little roadside pool;
Sleeps the butterfly on the weed,
Sleeps the drifted thistle-seed.
Like a great and blazing gem,
Basks the beetle on the stem.
Up and down the shining rays
Dancing midges weave their maze."

* * * * *

The pencil with which Roberts sketches autumn scenes is equally deft and delicate:

"The morning sky is white with mist, the earth
   White with the inspiration of the dew.
   The harvest light is on the hills anew,
   And cheer in the grave acre's fruitful girth.
   Only in this high pasture is there dearth,
   Where the grey thistles crowd in ranks austere,
   As if the sod, close-cropt for many a year,
   Brought only bane and bitterness to birth."

* * * * *

"Purple, the narrowing alleys stretched between
   The spectral shooks, a purple harsh and cold,
   But spotted, where the gadding pumpkins run,
   With bursts of blaze that startle the serene
   Like sudden voices, — globes of orange bold,
   Elate to mimic the unrisen sun."

These passages, only a few from the many in which Roberts has recorded for us the various aspects of the Canadian year, make it indubitably clear that he has few equals as a descriptive artist among Canadian writers.

CHAPTER 22

BLISS CARMAN
(1861-1929)

Bliss Carman was born at Fredericton, New Brunswick, of Loyalist descent. His mother was Sophia Bliss, and on the Bliss side he was a first cousin of Charles G. D. Roberts and a distant cousin of Ralph Waldo Emerson. He received his first education from his father, a barrister by profession. He attended the Collegiate School at Fredericton, where his interest in letters was first aroused by the head-master, later known to the world as Sir George Parkin. From the Collegiate School Carman proceeded to the University of New Brunswick, from which he graduated in 1881 with honours in Latin and Greek and a gold medal for Latin prose. Following his graduation he spent a year at home in private reading and then spent a year in study at Edinburgh University. Subsequent to his return to Fredericton in 1884, he studied law, taught school under Parkin, and worked at field engineering. From 1886 to 1888 he studied at Harvard University with a view to teaching English literature. After leaving Harvard, he spent his winters chiefly in New York, in Washington, and at New Canaan, Connecticut, and his summers chiefly in Nova Scotia, in the Catskills, on Nantucket Island, and at Scituate, Massachusetts. His life was further varied by a walking tour in England and France, and by visits to Canada, to the Bahama Islands, and to California. During the winter of 1919-20 he suffered a serious break-down in health, from which he recovered after a sufficient period of rest. The interest in his work has steadily increased since this illness, so that Carman, formerly a poet of the chosen few, has become in large measure a household poet. The interest in his poetry was greatly stimulated by his extensive lecture and reading tours in the United States and in Canada in the years following his recovery. A competent scholar and critic as well as a creative artist, Carman edited the *Oxford Book of American Verse* (1927) and was engaged on a new edition of the *Oxford Book of Canadian Verse* at the time of his death.

Carman's poetry has so completely overshadowed his prose that students of Canadian literature other than specialists in the field are scarcely aware of the existence of the latter. Carman's prose is chiefly the result of his editorial and journalistic work, from 1890 to 1895, for such publications as the New York *Independent, Current Literature,* the *Atlantic Monthly,* the *Chap Book* (Chicago), and, above all, the *Boston Transcript.* From his contributions to the last were largely made up his *The Kinship of Nature* (1904), *The Friendship of Art* (1904), and *The Poetry of*

[179]

Life (1905). In *The Making of Personality* (1908), he collaborated with Mrs. Mary Perry King, wife of Dr. Morris King, both old friends of Carman, with whom he was staying at the time of his death. *Talks on Poetry and Life* (1926) is the outcome of lectures to Canadian students on Canadian literature. These five volumes, with an essay on James Whitcomb Riley, constitute Carman's prose work in book form. His prose is clear and makes a simple appeal to the intellect rather than to the emotions. It is valuable chiefly as a key to the meaning of his poetry.

Carman began writing original verse not long after he had gone to Harvard. About the time that he formed with Richard Hovey at Harvard the friendship that induced him to give up teaching for poetry and that later resulted in the three volumes of the *Songs from Vagabondia* series, Carman's style came under the influence of that of his cousin, C. G. D. Roberts, then Professor of English at the University of King's College, Windsor, Nova Scotia, with whom he spent several summers. The period during which Carman published poetry extends over more than thirty-five years, and during that time he produced a considerable body of poetic material.

There are two difficulties in the way of adequate appreciation of Carman's poetry. One is that in assembling poems for a volume he consciously worked on the principle of bringing together in one book poems that are similar in mood or tone, with the result that for many readers there is an effect of monotony. The other difficulty is that the great body of Carman's verse falls into three distinctly marked periods, the recognition of which demands more than a casual reading and is made more difficult by the principle of collection just mentioned.

Carman's first or romantic period is represented by the poetry written before the publication of *Behind the Arras: A Book of the Unseen* (1895). It is only natural that in this period, which included the years of his vigorous young manhood, he should manifest in a higher degree than in any later period that highly sensitized response to the world about him without which he could not have been a creative artist. His senses and emotions are ever alert and responsive to the many stimuli that come to him from without; he has life and he has it abundantly. The mere living is an experience of such rich joy that he is compelled to the attempt to share his transports with others through the medium of poetry. He has the gift of expression so far as effective imagery and verbal music are concerned, but so intense, rich, and varied is his response to life and so exuberant is his imagination that he is overwhelmed by the wealth of experience that seems worthy of utterance. When all of life seems good, it is difficult to make a selection. Hence it is that in this period he produced work that, however much it is characterized by verbal music and emotional and imaginative power, is also characterized at times by the obscurity or paucity of meaning and by the inartistic form or even formlessness that result from the undisciplined outpouring of the experiences of a highly sensitive nature depending

[181]

for its effects upon accumulation of details rather than upon selection, one of the cardinal principles of art.

Carman, being a genius, did not remain satisfied with the mere joy of living, however ecstatic his enjoyment of life might be. He found it necessary not only to feel life but also to meditate upon its meaning. The careful reader of *Behind the Arras* will find reflected in it a period of transitional brooding by means of which the poet passed from an emotional to a philosophical attitude toward life. The excessive romanticism of the first period gives way to the equally excessive rationalism of the second period. In this period the poet formulates his philosophy of life, hence the rationalism. So pleased was he with his new metaphysical point of view that, as in the case with the joy of life in the first period, he sought to communicate it to others through the medium of literary art; hence the didacticism of his second period. Although the expression of philosophical ideas in artistic form is the most difficult task the man of letters can attempt, Carman stood to gain in the process by the tempering of imagination with reason. The work of the second period shows the predomination of reason over imagination so far as content is concerned, but on the formal side there is still occasional artistic weakness through lack of selection and condensation, even after the poet turned to the ancient classics for material and models.

The third and most artistic period of Carman's work, his classical period, came when imagination, temporarily usurped by reason in the second period, regained, not the absolute sway of the first period, but a balanced, tempered rule, and when the poet, by continued attention to the classics, attained to mastery of expression. In this period the poetic material is the product of imagination most happily wedded to reason, and though it may at times be excessively condensed, in striking contrast with the over-abundant detail of the first period, it is always expressed in excellent form.

The recognition of the principle on which Carman brought poems together in a book and of the three periods into which his work falls, removes the chief obstacles to the appreciation of his poetry. What seems at first sight to be a bewildering difficulty to the student of Carman's poetry is the number of volumes in which his poetry appeared. This apparent difficulty vanishes with the knowledge that the ordinary student of Canadian literature can get a reasonably adequate acquaintance with Carman from two volumes, *Ballads and Lyrics* (1923), selected from six of his earlier books of poetry, and *Later Poems* (1921), made up chiefly of poems taken from the last three volumes preceding its publication. After these two representative collections appeared, Carman published three more volumes of poetry, *Far Horizons* (1925), *Wild Garden* (1929), and *Sanctuary* (1929). Interesting as these three later publications are, to show the extent to which Carman retained his poetic gift to the last, they are not an indispensable supplement to the representative volumes to which reference has been made.

[183]

The reader of these two volumes will detect the grounds on which it has been contended that Carman is Canada's major poet, whether or not he accepts the contention as being established. No one can read many poems by Carman before he is impressed with the poet's musical gift. He sings because he must, and he does it as spontaneously as do the birds. It may be true that at times in the work of his first period his music is cloying because he "sings on and on", but this is of small import in comparison with the fact that he is able to sustain the sweetness of his lyrical lilt throughout such a great body of poetry. Singing is not his only gift; he can also paint word-pictures. While he has not written so large a quantity of excellent description of nature in verse as have Roberts and Lampman, he has done some of it exceedingly well. He is more concerned with interpreting nature than with painting it in words. One of the most significant characteristics of his work is the way in which he interprets the universe in terms of joy, love, truth, and beauty. Through these, especially the last, he experiences God. In *Vestigia* he seeks God and finds Him in the response of his senses to the beauty manifested in the world about him.

In brief, Carman's fame depends on his achievement as a verbal melodist, descriptive artist, and philosophical poet.

CHAPTER 23

WILLIAM WILFRED CAMPBELL
(1861-1919)

Campbell was of the same stock as the dukes of Argyll, the novelist Henry Fielding, and the poet Thomas Campbell. He was the son of Rev. Thomas Campbell, who, at the time of Wilfred's birth was rector of the Anglican church at Berlin (now Kitchener), Ontario. The poet's earliest years were spent in different parts of eastern Ontario. When he was about ten years of age, his father moved to Wiarton, situated in the midst of beautiful natural surroundings on Georgian Bay. Wiarton became the family home, and the beauty and romance of the neighbourhood exercised an important influence in shaping the young man's imagination. His education, begun at home, was continued at Owen Sound High School, and, after two years of teaching, at the University of Toronto where he began the Arts course, but at the beginning of his second academic year, registered as a theological student at Wycliffe College. He spent one year at Wycliffe and then became a special student at the Episcopal Divinity School, Cambridge, Massachusetts. He married in 1884, was ordained in 1885, and

[185]

spent three years in pastoral work in New England. He returned to Canada in 1888 as rector of Trinity Church, St. Stephen, New Brunswick, where he remained two years. In 1890 he moved to Southampton, Ontario, not far from Wiarton, his boyhood home. After a few months in Southampton, feeling the restraint that the dogmas of his Church put on his freedom of speech, he gave up the ministry, the profession of both his father and his grandfather, and entered the Civil Service at Ottawa, his appointment being the last made by Sir John A. Macdonald. In the Service were also Archibald Lampman and Duncan Campbell Scott, with whom Campbell for a time conducted a literary department of the Toronto *Globe*. Other friendships at Ottawa were a great stimulus to his literary work, to which his outwardly uneventful life enabled him quietly to devote his leisure until the shadows of the Great War darkened his soul. Soon after the coming of peace restored his spirits, he died of pneumonia.

Campbell early attempted both verse and prose. During his three years of parish work in New England he began to contribute poems to such magazines as *Harper's* and *The Atlantic Monthly*. He found much of literary inspiration in his sojourn at St. Stephen, and worked at his poetry with earnest zeal. A slight volume entitled *Snowflakes and Sunbeams* appeared during his first year at St. Stephen, and the poems of this volume, with others added, made up the volume entitled *Lake Lyrics,* published in the following year, while he was still at St. Stephen. Other volumes followed at more or less regular intervals from the time of his Civil Service appointment to the outbreak of the Great War.

Campbell's prose need not detain us long. His production of prose was incidental and relatively insignificant. His contribution to fiction includes two historical novels, *Ian of the Orcades* (1906) and *A Beautiful Rebel* (1909), a reading of which shows that his narrative style is without distinction. His descriptive prose is exemplified in *Canada* (1907). While there are passages in this book that do something to bring the beauty of Canada to us through the medium of the printed page, Campbell's description is mainly of the type to be found in guide-books.

Poetry was his natural medium of expression, but even in it he frequently strikes a "jarring lyre", especially in matters of rhythm and of adaptation of verse movement and rhyme schemes to lyric mood. These discords are to be expected from his theory that "the spirit and not the form makes earth's literature". His early acknowledgment of Tennyson as his master, therefore, must be understood as applying to the content of his poetry rather than to the form; as is well known, Tennyson's poetry has immaculate form; Campbell's material shows the influence also of Wordsworth, Coleridge, Browning, and Arnold. That Campbell, under guidance of such masters, could have written poetry of consistently finished form had it not been for the much higher estimation in which he held content than form, is manifest from a consideration of his poetry of various kinds.

His early descriptive nature lyrics show that he was

[187]

capable of writing poetry that would rank with the best
of its kind in this field. A few brief extracts will show the
effectiveness of diction whether he is writing pictorial or
atmospheric description:—

"The sunbeams fall in golden flakes,
Like snow-banks flamed the clouds are furled;
The soft light shakes
On wave that breaks
On wave, far round the gleaming world.

Great brown, bare rocks, wet, purple dyed
By sunsets' beams, hedge in this realm
Of sky and wide,
Bleak sweep of tide,
Grey, tossed, scarce-ploughed by keel or helm."

Beside this September sunset on Lake Huron may be set
an October scene:—

"Bright, pallid, changing, chill October morn:
Across your windy, keen exhilarant air,
You loom, a cameo dream, a vision fair;
Where through your purples and mauves of skeleton
    trees,
Friezes of lingering foliage, russet browns,
And wine-like crimsons, flaming torches, gold
Of maples, beeches, sumachs, poplars, shine
The horn-like, cloudy windows of the sky."

How skilfully, too, the poet suggests two aspects of autumn
in two adjacent stanzas:—

"On this grey autumn morn of haunted sadness,
   All wrecked of wind and rain;

* * * * *

Glad leaves, all ruddy, russet, green and golden,
   Across my pathway hurled".

If there are any artistic defects in these passages descriptive
of nature in Canada, they are in the handling of metre and
rhyme, and not in the choice of words.

From his early descriptive nature lyrics, which show
an appreciation of nature for its own sake that challenges
comparison with the British romantic poets and with Roberts
and Lampman, Campbell soon passed to poems of intense
emotional appeal, occasionally with a Coleridgian atmosphere,
and to poems of philosophic reflection on human life, in
which Nature, because of her kinship with man, at various
times soothes, consoles, cheers, and stimulates, but rarely,
except in a few of the posthumously published poems, re-
appears merely because of her own beauty.

No Canadian poet has sought more earnestly than Campbell to penetrate the mystery of life and find its meaning.
In his quest for the meaning of life he, somewhat like
Emerson, depends for truth, not upon the logical processes
of the mind, but upon the soul, aided at the lowest by a

blind instinct or impulse and at the highest by "insight". For the spiritual energy essential to the strenuous quest for the knowledge of the meaning of life he depends upon the power of love.

The reflective reader naturally inquires as to the results of Campbell's method of seeking the truth about the reason of our being here. The answer seems to be that, in spite of the poet's condemnation of the materialism that accepts only empiric and reasoned truth and of his exaltation of the idealism that accepts intuitive spiritual truth, he was not wholly satisfied with the wisdom attained by intuition, for there is throughout his poetry an undertone of sadness at the absence of logical proof for things spiritual. This is particularly noticeable in poems coloured by the thought that death, for Campbell the unsolved mystery, may mean, notwithstanding his intuitional belief in immortality, annihilation of his life-loving soul. He was very sensitive, he had a great zest for life, so much so that the prospect of possible annihilation was a very gloomy one, and it may be that his characteristic melancholy was largely the result of his failing to find what would be to him satisfying logical proof of his most cherished ideas about life as derived by the process of intuition.

A person of such keenly responsive senses and emotions will have dramatic power if he be capable of understanding other people's emotions as he understands his own. Campbell's ability to enter into the emotional crises of others was early revealed in his narrative poems, and some of his situations in these poems are presented with great dramatic power. This power is revealed in poems of various kinds, such as "Dan'l and Mat", "Lazarus", and the unforgettable dramatic monologue "Unabsolved".

Campbell displayed in his dramatic work the three outstanding characteristics of his lyric and narrative poems — intense emotion, gloomy atmosphere, and persistent endeavour to interpret life. He follows Mair in casting his dramas in poetical form on the Shakespearian model, but he is distinctive among the Canadian imitators of Shakespeare in writing philosophical drama or drama of ideas. Because of his interest in expounding through his dramatic compositions a philosophy of life, he chose historical characters, or at least such as had been made the subject of previous literary treatment. Thus we find him writing a play on the Arthurian material. In his poetical dramas his characters are moulded on heroic proportions, and, there, central problems are usually made to have a significant bearing on the problems of modern times. As a philosophical dramatist he has considerable skill in bringing out the dramatic situations that arise from the conflict of contradictory philosophies or from the effect on individuals of principles of conduct imposed upon them by organized social power.

The insistent note of Campbell's teaching whether in reflective or dramatic poetry is that the only sure foundation of human welfare is the cultivation of high ideals. This insistence is specially manifest in his patriotic verse. He dwells lovingly on the thought of Canada as a nation, but not as

[191]

a nation unto herself, for he has a vision of a higher destiny for Canada as a nation within the Empire, and this vision is linked up with his interest in preserving civilization through the inculcation of high ideals, since it was his firm conviction that on the righteousness of Canada and the Empire depend their destiny and that of civilization.

Chapter 24

EMILY PAULINE JOHNSON
(1862-1913)

E. Pauline Johnson (Tekahionwake) occupies a unique place among outstanding Canadian writers in that she was the daughter of a white mother and an Indian father. This fact raises the question as to whether her literary success can in any manner be attributed to her Indian blood. Are the Indians an artistic people in general or a literary people in particular?

No race, however primitive, could have occupied for untold generations a continent like North America without discovering or inventing some means of satisfying the needs of life other than the physical, and the American Indians did find ways of furnishing themselves with social, intellectual, spiritual, and aesthetic satisfaction. Their literature, which is our especial concern here, is of particular interest. It consisted of unwritten legends and folk-tales recorded in the memory of raconteurs and passed on from generation to generation by oral tradition. Fortunately for the student of Indian culture, a great deal of this material has been

[193]

taken down and preserved through the medium of the printed page.

One would suppose that the conditions of Indian life in North America would tend to the starkest kind of realism, yet the most striking characteristic of Indian literature in general is its romantic quality. For the Indians, "the earth swarmed with spiritual powers and presences, gods and demi-deities." (Pierce). A notable English rendering of Algonquin literary material is Silas T. Rand's *Legends of the Micmacs* (1894). The stories in this collection indicate the extent to which magicians and giants, transformations, and other supernatural phenomena were employed as literary *motifs* by the Micmac family of the Algonquin tribe. The romantic quality of the Indians' imagination is reflected also in their systems of theology and cosmology and in their myths of creation, some of the latter of which compare very favourably with similar material in other literatures.

Somewhat nearer to the reality of the visible world are Indian epic legends, which, though obviously furnishing a kind of escape from reality or of wish fulfilment, are built up around heroes whose feats are not very much more supernatural than those of the epic heroes of less primitive peoples. Of these epic heroes of Indian literature a very interesting one is Glooscap, who is the central figure in several of the legends in Rand's collection. He lived in a very large wigwam on Cape Blomidon. His status as an epic personage is well summed up by Helen L. Webster in her introduction to Rand's volume: "He was, to say the least, almost an object of worship. He looked and lived like other men; he ate, drank, smoked, slept, and danced along with them. But he never died, never was sick, never grew old." Further, the Indians suppose that he is still alive and that he will return to the scene of his former activities. The parallel in this last respect between Glooscap and such heroes as King Arthur and Barbarossa is very striking.

Most important of Indian epic characters, of course, is Hiawatha, whose name Longfellow has made known to the literary world. The Hiawatha material is of the class of epic legend that has as its core an element of historical fact. The historical Hiawatha was a Mohawk chieftain of the sixteenth century who effected the Iroquois confederation known to students of American history as the Five Nations. Iroquois legend attributed to him supernatural powers, and he, bearing a different name among different tribes, became in the tradition of the North American Indians a culture hero "of miraculous birth, who was sent among them to clear their rivers, forests, and fishing-grounds, and to teach them the arts of peace." (Longfellow). In a volume of Schoolcraft, one of the best authorities on the North American Indians, Longfellow found the Iroquois form of the Hiawatha tradition as recorded from the oral narration of an Onondaga chief. Into this tradition the poet wove "other curious Indian legends", also drawn chiefly from Schoolcraft. Longfellow made Hiawatha a hero of the Ojibwas, who belong to the Algonquin tribe, and so Longfellow's Hiawatha is a tribal brother of Glooscap, the Indian epic hero of the region made famous by Longfellow's other most widely known poem, *Evangeline*.

Cursory as are the foregoing glimpses into the fascinating realm of Indian literature, they are sufficient to show that he would be a bold man who would say that Pauline Johnson owed none of her literary ability to her Indian blood. Through her father, G. H. M. Johnson (Onwanonsyshon), Head Chief of the Six Nations Indians, like Hiawatha a Mohawk chief, she was descended from a Blood Royal line that went back four hundred years, and her grandfather Johnson, famous for his colourful oratory, was known as "the Mohawk warbler." Her mother was Emily S. Howells, a cousin of William Dean Howells, one of the most famous novelists of the United States.

Pauline Johnson was born on her father's estate, "Chief-swood", on the Six Nations' Reserve, near Brantford, Ontario. Her formal education was meagre. For two years she was under the tutelage of a nursery governess, for three years she attended an Indian day school near "Chiefswood", and for two years she was a pupil at Central School, Brantford. This slight formal training was supplemented by considerable experience of outdoor life and by a wide range of reading. Poetry constituted a large part of her reading, and she had read Scott, Longfellow, Byron, and Shakespeare before she was twelve years of age. She had begun to make jingles even before she had learned to write. Eventually some of her poems began to appear in such magazines as

Gems of Poetry, New York, and Professor Goldwin Smith's *The Week,* Toronto. The attention attracted by these poems led to the most fateful event in the shaping of her career.

In 1892, when she was thirty years of age, she was invited, along with other poets, to read some of her own work at a poetry evening held by the Toronto Young Liberal Club. Her reply to this invitation is rich in human interest and helps to establish the truth of the poet's observation that the colonel's lady and Judy O'Grady are sisters under the skin. This Indian sister wrote back that she was scared to death at the thought of appearing before a high-brow Toronto audience, she having never recited outside the walls of her own home, and that she had not a suitable dress for the occasion. Nevertheless she came, she recited, and she conquered. So great was her success that she was immediately launched on a sea of public recitals, the proceeds of which were to help her find a market for her poetry. During the next two years she earned, by a series of recitals throughout Canada, the means to go to London, England, and publish her first volume of poems there.

For sixteen years, in addition to writing poetry, she continued to give recitals, in the United States, Canada, Newfoundland, and the British Isles. Her success on the public platform was no doubt partly due to her mixed blood and to the fact that she wore at her recitals the attire of the Indian nation to which she belonged — Mohawk jewellery, a dagger, and a necklace of the claws of the cinnamon bear — but it was due chiefly to the spontaneous naturalness of her art in reading. Enjoyable as was the success of her recitals wherever she went, she was not strong enough to endure the strain that the labour and the inconveniences of travel threw upon her, and when her health failed she settled at Vancouver, British Columbia, where, as far as failing health would permit, with the indomitable spirit that characterized her she devoted the rest of her life to literature.

Her work in prose has a twofold interest. It includes entertaining tales for boys and girls. These tales, on Indian themes, were published in two volumes in 1913, and both volumes were reprinted in 1926. More interesting still is the material in *Legends of Vancouver* (1911). While in London in 1906, Miss Johnson met the late Chief Joe Capilano, of Vancouver, when he visited England and was received at Buckingham Palace by King Edward VII and Queen Alexandra. So pleased was the Chief at the ability of our Indian poet to greet him in the Chinook tongue that a friendship was formed as a result of which he told her a series of tales that had not hitherto been revealed to any English-speaking person. These tales, which show the poetic imagination and lofty moral idealism of the Coast Indians, Miss Johnson sympathetically recorded in rhythmical prose, with artistic reproduction of the setting. *Legends of Vancouver,* of which there was a new, revised, and illustrated edition in 1922, does for the literature of the Indians of the Pacific Coast a somewhat similar service to that done by Rand's *Legends of the Micmacs* for the literature of the Indians of the Atlantic region.

As a result of her early practice in the composition of verse, Miss Johnson was writing creditable poems at the age of twelve years, and by the time she published her first volume her art was mature. Except for a few dramatic monologues, she rarely based a poem wholly on the experiences of white men. She sometimes described Indian characters in a background of nature; more frequently and more effectively she introduced them in emotional poems based on tribal enmity or on the injustice of the white man to the Indian. And yet the careful student of her poetry can trace a marvellous broadening of her emotional range. Her outlook broadens from the Indian to the Canadian, from the Canadian to the Imperial, and from the Imperial to the cosmopolitan, in which her sympathy is as broad as the human race.

The chief merits of her style are verbal music, suggestive of Swinburne, resulting from skill in metre, rhyme, alliteration, assonance, and vowel and consonant sequences of rare melodic quality; and poetic description, with refreshing originality in diction and figures of speech, of Canadian nature. Her skill in both music and description are suggested by the following stanzas from "In the Shadows":—

"On the water's idle pillow
Sleeps the overhanging willow,
Green and cool;
Where the rushes lift their burnished
Oval heads from out the tarnished
Emerald pool.
Where the very silence slumbers,
Water-lilies grow in numbers,
Pure and pale;
All the morning they have rested,
Amber crowned, and pearly crested,
Fair and frail."

CHAPTER 25

ARCHIBALD LAMPMAN
(1861-99)

The relatively large amount of biographical and critical writing about Lampman since his death is indicative of his greatness as a poet. In the year following his death, his poems were published with a memoir by Duncan Campbell Scott, himself one of the greatest of Canadian poets. In 1926 a new Lampman volume, entitled *Lyrics of the Earth, Sonnets and Ballads,* was published under the direction of Scott, who furnished new and more intimate biographical and critical material, as compared with that in the former edition. Scott is responsible also for the Lampman volume of the Makers of Canadian Literature series. In 1927 Norman Gregor Guthrie ("John Crichton") published a volume entitled *The Poetry of Archibald Lampman,* and in 1929 C. Y. Connor, a Canadian by birth, now head of the department of English at Sweet Briar College, Virginia, published a biographical and critical volume entitled *Archibald Lampman: A Canadian Poet of Nature.*

For a poetic career Lampman was fortunate both in heredity and environment. Not only was he of superior family on both his father's and his mother's side, the former of Pennsylvania-Dutch Loyalist descent, the latter of Knickerbocker Loyalist and Irish ancestry, but he was also the son of parents whose gifts were complementary. From his father he inherited his logical power, his accuracy of observation, and his rare gift of expression; from his mother, his poetic temperament. He was born at Morpeth, Ontario, where his father was rector. When the boy was in his sixth year, the family moved, first to Perrytown and then to Gore's Landing, on the shore of Rice Lake. There for several of his most impressionable years Lampman absorbed the beauty of his surroundings, thus becoming fitted because of his environment for his supreme literary achievement, poetry of Canadian nature.

His education, begun by his father, was continued from 1870 to 1874 at a good private school, and then, through the heroic efforts of his mother and the aid of scholarships, at the Collegiate Institute, Cobourg, whither the family moved, at Trinity College School, Port Hope, and at Trinity College, Toronto, from which the poet graduated in 1882 with second-class honours in classics. After a few months of unsatisfactory high-school teaching, he became a clerk in the Post Office Department of the Civil Service at Ottawa, a position which he held for the rest of his life.

While at college Lampman wrote both prose and verse for the college papers, contemplated a novel, and attempted epic poetry. Campbell tells us that Wordsworth, Arnold, and Keats were the "high masters" of Lampman's song.

A reading of his narrative poems, though they have some of the merits of the successful narrative poems of Wordsworth and Arnold, nevertheless shows that he was wise in abandoning his epic intentions and cultivating his lyric genius, for he did his best work in descriptive and lyric poetry of nature.

Throughout his poetic career Lampman wrote descriptions of Canadian nature that excel in rich sensuousness and felicity of diction. The following extracts, which one reluctantly separates from the perfect wholes of which they form a part, illustrate not only Lampman's excellence in description but also the uniformity of that excellence for any season of the year and afford a basis of comparison with the descriptive poetry of Roberts, in connection with the study of whom a parallel list of extracts was furnished.

In a poem entitled "A January Morning", Lampman writes thus:

"And here behind me come the woodmen's sleighs
    With shouts and clamorous squeakings; might and
    main
    Up the steep slope the horses stamp and strain,
    Urged on by hoarse-tongued drivers—cheeks ablaze,
    Iced beards and frozen eyelids—team by team,
    With frost-fringed flanks, and nostrils jetting steam."

Equally effective is another etching of a decidedly different winter scene, in "Winter Evening":

"Tonight the very horses springing by
  Toss gold from whitened nostrils. In a dream
  The streets that narrow to the westward gleam
  Like rows of golden palaces; and high
  From all the crowded chimneys tower and die
  A thousand aureoles. Down in the west
  The brimming plains beneath the sunset rest,
  One burning sea of gold."

The approach of spring is pictured thus in "In March":

"The sun falls warm: the southern winds awake:
  The air seethes upwards with a steamy shiver:
  Each dip of the road is now a crystal lake,
  And every rut a little dancing river.
        *   *   *   *   *
  The last seared drifts are eating fast away
  With glassy tinkle into glittering laces:
  Dogs lie asleep, and little children play
  With tops and marbles in the sun-bare places . . . . "

"April" furnishes a vivid picture of spring more advanced:

"The old year's cloaking of brown leaves, that bind
  The forest floor-ways, plated close and true —
  The last love's labour of the autumn wind —
  Is broken with curled flower buds white and blue
  In all the matted hollows, and speared through
  With thousand serpent-spotted blades upsprung
  Yet bloomless, of the slender adder-tongue."

[204]

"Nesting Time" has some felicitous spring touches:

> "And all the twigs and branches of the birch
> Are shooting into tiny emerald flames:
>
> * * * * *
>
> The gold-green poplar, jocund as may be,
> The sunshine in its laughing heart receives,
> And shimmers in the wind innumerably
> Through all its host of little lacquered leaves."

A consummately beautiful description of a summer scene is found in "Heat", which begins:

> "From plains that reel to southward, dim,
> The road runs by me white and bare;
> Up the steep hill it seems to swim
> Beyond, and melt into the glare.
> Upward half-way, or it may be
> Nearer the summit, slowly steals
> A hay-cart, moving dustily
> With idly clacking wheels.
>
> By his cart's side the wagoner
> Is slouching slowly at his ease,
> Half-hidden in the windless blur
> Of white dust puffing to his knees.

How effectively Lampman could represent in words the gorgeous pageantry of the Canadian autumn is well shown in "September", from which the following lines are taken:

"In far-off russet corn-fields, where the dry
Grey shocks stand peaked and withering, half concealed
In the rough earth, the orange pumpkins lie,
Full-ribbed; and in the windless pasture-field
The sleek red horses o'er the sun-warmed ground
Stand pensively about in companies,
While all around them from the motionless trees
The long clean shadows sleep without a sound.

Under cool elm trees floats the distant stream,
Moveless as air; and o'er the vast warm earth
The fathomless daylight seems to stand and dream,
A liquid cool elixir — all its girth
Bound with faint haze, a frail transparency,
Whose lucid purple barely veils and fills
The utmost valleys and the thin last hills,
Nor mars one whit their perfect clarity.

It must not be supposed that Lampman can do nothing but record in felicitous phrase the atmospheric and pictorial aspects of Canadian nature. In his attitude to nature he resembles Wordsworth. For Lampman nature is sometimes merely earth, more frequently a great universal mother, like the Demeter of Greek mythology. He finds in nature beauty, comfort, and consolation; stimulus to dreams, which for him are highly significant, in fact are the essential reality; a source of intuitive wisdom, of wisdom "won without a quest", a consideration of importance, since "Life is not all for effort"; kinship between nature's spirit

and his own soul. The physical beauty and spiritual significance which he finds in nature he is able, like Wordsworth,
by his felicity of phrase, to communicate to his readers in
proportion to their aesthetic susceptibility.

Lampman's successful poetry is not confined to poems
that describe and interpret nature. He wrote also reflective
poems, some of which were stimulated by contact with
nature, and others of which sprang from a stimulus apart
from nature. In either case his reflections, though not of
great profundity, are pleasing and edifying, and they are
expressed with the felicity of diction that characterizes his
nature poetry. His reflective poetry is most frequently cast
in the sonnet form, usually one of the most thoughtful of
lyric forms, and is well exemplified by "Truth", "Knowledge", and "The Larger Life". Further, some of his later
poems are atmospheric representations of imagined lands
or characters. In these he is not so successful with atmosphere as he is in poems based on actual Canadian nature.

In short, whatever degree of success Lampman attained
in the different kinds of poetry that he attempted, he is
always most effective in poems that exemplify his marvellous
skill in describing pictorially or atmospherically Canadian
scenes and in transmitting to his readers his rapturous enjoyment of the beauty and meaning thereof, and these poems
have deservedly won for him the rank of Canada's greatest
nature poet.

[207]

CHAPTER 26

FREDERICK GEORGE SCOTT
(1861-........)

Frederick George Scott is the son of parents of English
birth. His father, Dr. William Edward Scott, was for nearly
forty years Professor of Anatomy at McGill University.
The poet was born at Montreal, and after attending the
high school there, proceeded to Bishop's College, Lennoxville, from which he received the degree of Master of
Arts in 1884. He was ordained a deacon in the same year,
and two years later became a priest. From 1886 to 1887
he held a curacy at Coggeshall, Essex, England, during
which period he attended King's College, London. On his
return to Canada he became rector of Drummondville,
Quebec, whence in 1896 he moved to the City of Quebec,
first as curate and then as rector of St. Matthews and later
(from 1906 on) as canon and archdeacon of Holy Trinity
Cathedral. His incumbency of the latter was temporarily
broken by his participation in the Great War, in which
service he held the high rank of Major and Senior Chaplain
of the First Canadian Division. He was beloved by the
men in the ranks, so much so that even today the enthusiasm

[208]

with which they speak of him has lost none of its glow, and in official recognition of his bravery and distinguished service he was awarded the D.S.O. and the C.M.G. and made an Honorary Lieutenant-Colonel.

Archdeacon Scott's work has not been restricted to the poetic field. In 1892 he published a piece of prose fiction entitled *Elton Hazelwood*. Though this is the work of a thinker rather than of a narrative artist, it shows at times his power in dramatic situations, a gift more fully manifested in his poetry. In 1922 he published *The Great War as I Saw it,* a volume which, in addition to illustrating further his accomplishment in narrative, shows the unostentatious effectiveness of his descriptive prose, a good example being his contrasting pictures of Valcartier in 1914 and 1919.

Archdeacon Scott has been called "The Poet of the Laurentians". To take this description as representatively characteristic would be as far from the truth as to regard Campbell as "The Poet of the Great Lakes" because of his *Lake Lyrics*. Scott, like Campbell, is essentially a philosophical poet. And there is far less excuse for failing to recognize him as such than there would be for a similar failure in the case of Campbell, for although the latter began to write about specific objects in nature and then became interested primarily in poetical expressions of his philosophy of life, Scott began as a philosopher and in the course of his artistic career has proceeded from the abstract, the general, and the universal to the concrete, the specific, and the particular.

[209]

Scott's first volume of poetry, *The Soul's Quest* (1888), contains chiefly philosophical poems that aim to solve the problems of life by the application of great religious principles. In "Catholicism" he admits that each religious system has made some contribution to an adequate philosophy of life, but in general he is an exponent of Christianity as the way of abundant life. The whole volume is pervaded by the personality of Jesus, and the title poem represents the soul as seeking rest in tomorrow and yesterday and not finding it, but finding peace in sacrificial service today. The Christian ideal thus set forth in the title poem of his first volume of poetry he chose as the supreme ideal of life to present to the soldiers at Valcartier. In his poetic Christian philosophy of life there is no trace of the mediaevalist or obscurantist. Like Tennyson, he deals with the problems of life in the full light of modern scientific knowledge, with all its emphasis on change according to law. His poem entitled "Evolution", for example, treats in a Tennysonian manner the problems of life and death, and the poet, taking into account the scientific knowledge of the day, finds his proof of immortality in the highest characteristic of man, individuality.

Scott's second volume of poems, *My Lattice* .. (1894), is also concerned with fundamental principles of life. It marks an artistic advance in imaginative power, in that the diction is more concrete, and in intensity of emotion, especially in poems that reveal a dramatic imagination akin to that of Browning. Among the best of these dramatic pieces are "Samson", "The Abbot", and "The Feud", the last of which is a successful attempt in the ballad manner. Some of the poems in this volume are written to give literary expression to definite philosophical ideas. Thus "Thor" employs Scandinavian material to symbolize the Christian doctrine of redemption; "Natura Victrix" tells us that if we would be one with nature our rule of conduct should be, "Wrestle not with what must be". As sources of inspiration, nature and human love supplement religion:—

> Speak, O Lord, in voice of thunder, show Thy foot-
> steps on the deep,
> Pour Thy sunshine from the heavens on the blinded
> eyes that weep,
> Till the harmonies of nature and exalted human love
> Make the universe a mirror of the glorious God above.

In his *The Unnamed Lake* . . . (1897) Scott reached the high-water mark of his artistic achievement. This volume is concerned, not with the discussion of great life principles, but with the expression of specific intellectual and emotional experiences, and the poet was therefore better able to concentrate on the artistic aspects of his material, with a resultant advance in emotional power and in imaginative vividness through concreteness of diction.

Other volumes of poetry have followed, some of them reprints of poems formerly published supplemented by a few new poems, others made up of new poems. Side by side with the old themes several new ones have been introduced.

One of the most interesting of these is the theme of patriotism. Scott expresses in verse a feeling of national consciousness that gives to his poetry, otherwise largely cosmopolitan, a touch of Canadian colour. But Canada as a nation is such only as a part of the Empire, and some of Scott's most effective patriotic poetry is that in which he expresses his loyalty to the mother land. Both aspects of his patriotism received a great stimulus from his experience in the Great War, and as a result he wrote war poetry that compares favourably with that of a number of others. Since the War, his poetry has voiced the ideals of brotherhood and peace.

The foregoing remarks on the content of Scott's poetry are sufficient to establish the fact that so far as material is concerned he should be associated with Wilfred Campbell as a philosophical poet. Moreover, there are respects in which Scott surpasses Campbell. The latter, we remember, did not hold artistic form in high regard. As a consequence his work at times suffers because his material has not been given expression commensurate with its worth. Scott always strives to give his material the most artistic expression of which he is capable. Further than that, the language of his poetic art is broader in its appeal than that of Campbell, so that he reaches a larger public. One of the most delightful characteristics of his style is its charming simplicity. The ease with which Scott may be understood and appreciated by the ordinary reader naturally results from the spontaneous

aptness of the poet's images and figures of speech, as may
be shown by a few citations:—

"O poor, sad hearts that struggle on and wait,
Like shipwrecked sailors on a spar at sea,
Through deepening glooms, if haply, soon or late,
Some day-dawn glimmer of what is to be, ... "
"Justin"

"Hast thou not seen the tints unfold,
From earth, sky, sea, and setting sun,
When all the glare of day was done,
And melt in one long stream of gold?

So down the dim-lit glades of time,
Age after age, things divers blend,
Each working for the same great end,
And in its working each sublime."
"Catholicism"

"I rose at midnight and beheld the sky
Sown thick with stars, like grains of golden sand
Which God had scattered loosely from His hand
Upon the floorways of His house on high; . . . . . . "
"The Heaven of Love"

THE PILGRIMAGE

"Upward and onward day by day,
    Straight is the course and narrow the way,
    But others before us the path have trod,
    And the top of the hill is the Heart of God."

These quotations show that Scott speaks to us with the tongue of the artist, employing the language of the imagination. In estimating his rank as a poet this is the important consideration, and not whether we are or are not in intellectual agreement with the ideas to which he gives artistic expression. As an illustration of his art as well as an epitome of his poetic career we may well conclude our study of the poet with the "Inscription" to his first volume:—

"Day after day,
    As I have wandered thro' the fields of life —
    Gay, happy fields, bright with the sun and sky —
    Flower after flower
    Has bloomed beside my path;
    And I have gathered them, a long-loved handful,
    Which I offer now
    To the unpitying, cruel-laughing world.
    And some are gay,
    Sparkling with joy and the bright sun of hope;
    And some are sad,
    Dipped in the crimson of the setting sun,
    Or blasted by the cold of winter winds;
    But all the roots

Are down, far down, within the spirit's depths,
Amid the voiceless shadows of the soul,
And each has sprung
From the warm life-blood throbbing in my heart."

CHAPTER 27

DUNCAN CAMPBELL SCOTT
(1862-........)

Duncan Campbell Scott's mother was of Scottish ancestry. His father, the Reverend William Scott, was born in Lincoln, England, went to the United States in 1837, followed journalism there for a while, and then moved to an Indian mission in Ontario. The poet was born at Ottawa. He received his education in his father's library, at the various schools where his father was stationed as a preacher, at the public schools of Ottawa, and at Stanstead College. In 1879, on the nomination of Sir John A. Macdonald, he entered the Canadian Civil Service at Ottawa as a clerk in the Department of Indian Affairs, of which Department he was made Superintendent General in 1913, an office which he still holds. In 1899 he was made a fellow of the Royal Society of Canada, of which he has held the offices of president and honorary secretary. The first degree of Doctor of Letters ever granted by the University of Toronto was conferred on him in 1922. In May, 1927, the Royal Society of Canada conferred on him the

[216]

Lorne Pierce medal, in recognition of his outstanding contribution to Canadian literature, an honour which has been bestowed also on Carman and Roberts.

And Scott is worthy of all the recognition that he has received. In fact it is well to conclude our study of the group of major Canadian poets who were born in the sixties with a consideration of his literary work, for in it is supremely manifest that of which Canadian literature in general (there are isolated exceptions) stands in the greatest need, namely, artistic conscience. In Scott the manifestation is twofold. First, he has studied with critical care the best literature of the world, especially that in the English language, and has acquired in addition a discriminating appreciation of painting and music. His literary art rests, therefore, not only on a full understanding of the methods by which the best is attained in literature, but also on the supplementary aids of other arts. The value of his appreciation of music is ever-present for the reader of his poetry, and poems like "Madonna with Two Angels" surely owe something to his study of painting. Secondly, he is always a conscientious and painstaking literary technician, never publishing anything until he has given it the most artistic form of which his genius is capable, never sacrificing quality for quantity. with the result that from the very first there is rarely if ever the touch of the amateur, practically always the stroke of the master artist.

For a man who writes with such care and who never allows his artistic work to interfere with the faithful per-

[217]

formance of his duties as a civil servant, Scott has produced a notable amount of literature. His prose includes the critical work on Lampman to which reference was made in our study of that poet, a biography of John Graves Simcoe in the "Makers of Canada" series, one-act plays and two volumes of short stories. His biographical and critical material is written with the competency that we would expect from our knowledge of his high standards, and the one-act plays are pleasing evidence of his keen interest in drama. The two volumes of short stories are next in importance to his poetry in establishing his rank as a Canadian man of letters. The *Village of Viger* (1896) is a delightful collection of tales and vignettes of French-Canadian life. *The Witching of Elspie* (1923) is made up of tales reflecting pioneer conditions in the Hudson Bay region. Striking as is the contrast in the setting of the two collections of stories, both illustrate common characteristics of Scott's style in narrative fiction. Setting and atmosphere are always vividly presented, the characters are always realistically portrayed, and the plots, though slight, are always effective. In fact the plots of these short pieces of fiction may well serve as a criterion of a reader's taste, for they are on that highly artistic level in which the plot is what it is because the characters are what they are, and so will not be adequately appreciated by those for whom plot is the all-important thing and who demand thrills whether or not they are appropriate to the type of character represented. Naturally this class of readers will find more to their taste in the latter volume than in the former.

Our approach to Scott's poetry may very suitably be made through his descriptive verse. He takes us through the Canadian year, and by choosing some of his finest passages describing the seasons we can afford ourselves a basis of comparison in this respect with Roberts and Lampman:—

> "The wind plunges — then stops;
> And a column of leaves in a whirl,
> Like a dervish that spins — drops,
> With a delicate rustle,
> Falls into a circle that thins;
> The leaves creep away one by one,
> Hiding in hollows and ruts; . . . . . . "
>
> "Labour and the Angel"

> "The field pools gathered into frosted lace;
> An icy glitter lined the iron ruts,
> And bound the circle of the musk-rat huts; . . . . . "
> "The First Snow"

> "Now swoops the wind from every coign and crest;
> Like filaments of silver, ripped and spun,
> The snow reels off the drift-ridge in the sun;
> And smoky clouds are torn across the west,
> Clouds that would snow if they had time to rest; . . . "
> "March"

"Snowdrops now begin in snows,
    Crocuses to flush,
Gentle scilla buds and blows
    Nurtured in the slush;
All about, like tinkling bells,
    Falls the ice a-melting; . . . . . . "
                            "Madrigal"

"Far in the east the rain-clouds sweep and harry,
    Down the long haggard hills, formless and low,
Far in the west the shell-tints meet and marry,
    Piled grey and tender blue and roseate snow; . . . "
                        "Spring on Mattagami"

"Pallid saffron glows the broken stubble,
    Brimmed with silver lie the ruts,
    Purple the ploughed hill;
Down a sluice with break and bubble
    Hollow falls the rill;
Falls and spreads and searches, . . . "
                        "The Fifteenth of April"

"Like a silver ball for perfume,
    Floats the world, and swings
Drowsy with remembered odours
    Of a million springs."
                            "Spring Night"

"Last night a storm fell on the world
    From heights of drouth and heat,
The surly clouds for weeks were furled,
    The air could only sway and beat, ...

The poignard lightning searched the air,
    The thunder ripped the shattered gloom,
The rain came down with a roar like fire,
    Full-voiced and clamorous and deep, ... "
                    "A Summer Storm"

"Under the sky without a stain
    The long, ripe rippling of the grain;
Light broadcast from the golden oats
Over the blackberry fences floats."
                    "Madonna with Two Angels"

"Acres of gold wheat
    Stir in the sunshine,
Rounding the hilltop,
Crested with plenty,
Filling the valley,
Brimmed with abundance; . . . . "
                    "The Harvest"

[221]

"The morns are grey with haze and faintly cold,
The early sunsets arc the west with red;
The stars are misty silver overhead,
Above the dawn Orion lies outrolled.
Now all the slopes are slowly growing gold,
And in the dales a deeper silence dwells;
The crickets mourn with funeral flutes and bells,
For days before the summer had grown old."
                              "September"

This colourful pageant of the Canadian year, with all its pictorial and atmospheric vividness expressed in musical language, may be supplemented by "Songs of Four Seasons", in which the poet concentrates the essence of the Canadian seasons in four similarly constructed songs.

The felicitous phrasing and musical cadence that characterize Scott's descriptive verse prevail also in his poems of other types. Because of his care as an artist, the narrative poems in his successive volumes reveal a growing mastery of narrative technique, especially in developing the emotional possibilities of dramatic situations. He has written the one-act play in poetic form as well as in prose. His lyrics are the expression of fancy, of intense elemental emotions, or of deep reflection on life; they are sometimes dependent on, at other times independent of, nature as a stimulus to creative imagination. As a reflective poet, he has gradually approached his philosophical ideal, to see life steadily and to see it whole; as a literary artist he has increasingly at-

[222]

tained aptness of phrase and exquisiteness of musical cadence. The significance of his material and the excellence of his form, therefore, give him a place among the greatest of Canadian poets, and some regard him as the greatest. Whether or not he is our greatest poet, his poetry, to be adequately appreciated, calls for a more cultivated and refined taste than that of any other Canadian poet.

CHAPTER 28

OTHER POETS, TO SERVICE

Canadian writers, like those of other lands. may be divided into major and minor groups. This does not mean that the student of literature can afford to neglect the minor writers. In fact, during the earlier stages of development in the appreciation of literature, it may be more advantageous to spend time on the work of minor writers, because in it one may study the principles of literary art in simpler manifestations than in the work of major writers. We can readily see how minor artists achieve their effects, whereas there is often an element of the inexplicable in the productions of creative genius.

Canada has had a goodly representation of minor poets, too large a number, indeed, to be studied here in biographical and critical detail. Fortunately this is not necessary, since the important facts of their lives are already accessible in handbooks and since they can be appreciated without elaborate introductory critical preparation. Some of the minor poets of Canada, though older by varying numbers of years than the poets of the major group, began to write long enough after their more illustrious brethren to seem to belong to a younger generation. Some have written poetry only as an avocation. Some are of interest for special types of work or for distinctive aspects of their subject matter. Some show to what extent a poet can be made as well as born, by writing good verse largely as the result of devoted study of one or more favourite poets.

Theodore Harding Rand (1835-1900), though twenty-five years older than Roberts, did not publish his first volume of verse until near the end of the nineteenth century, and only three years before his death. He and William Douw Lighthall (1857-........), who in 1929 was appointed President of the Canadian Authors' Association, are worthy of remembrance in a special way as editors of anthologies of Canadian verse. Two women of more than ordinary interest, who, though born in the late fifties did not begin to publish verse till the nineties, are Agnes Ethelwyn Wetherald (1857-........) and Susie Frances (Riley) Harrison ("Seranus") (1859-........). The former reached the realm of literature by the route of journalism, one of the most common routes in modern times. Her verse is marked by graceful imagination, apt diction, and musical cadence, all exemplified in the familiar poem "The Pasture Field", in which, in four stanzas; she artistically records characteristic aspects of the four seasons of the year in Canada. Mrs. Harrison is significant as the compiler of the first anthology of Canadian verse and as an interpreter in verse of French-Canadian life. A third woman to reach ripe maturity before appearing in print is Helena Coleman (1860-........), who, though born in the same year as Roberts, did not publish a volume of verse till the twentieth century was well begun. Arthur Wentworth Hamilton Eaton (1849-........), eleven years older than Miss Coleman, did not publish his first volume of verse till the year preceding her first volume. Another belated bloom in verse was that of William E. Marshall (1859-1923), whose first volume appeared when he was fifty years of age. His work is worthy of attention not so much as the spontaneous outpouring of genius as an example of what can be done in a creative way by a devotee of poetry in general and of the work of Keats in particular.

Albert Durrant Watson (1859-1926) and Albert Ernest Stafford Smythe (1861-........) are of special interest among the philosophical poets of Canada as the exponents in verse of mystical spiritual monism.

Mysticism finds voice also in the verse of John Daniel Logan (1869-1929) and in that of Francis Sherman (1871-1926), whose work, evidently influenced by the Pre-Raphaelites, has not received adequate recognition for its quality, probably because it is relatively small in quantity. Sherman was born in Fredericton, New Brunswick, and spent a large part of his life there, a fact that associates him in our minds with Roberts and Carman, of whom he was a relative. For years Sherman was employed by the Royal Bank. After his marriage to a wealthy American woman, he gave up banking but did not as a result add any appreciable amount to his poetic output. He died at Atlantic

City. His hope of remembrance is *Matins* (1896), his only publication of sufficient bulk to be called a book, the beauty of the contents of which, in felicity of epithet and musical cadence, affords the reader many a delightful surprise.

Three women born in the sixties, who have not yet been discussed here or under other forms of literature, deserve mention for their verse. Mrs. Jean (McKishnie) Blewett (1862-........) writes of home associations in a simple way, so that her poems make a special appeal to women. Mrs. Annie Charlotte (Armitage) Dalton (1865-........) is of interest on the one hand for her successful modern adaptations of sixteenth and seventeenth century verse patterns, and on the other for the pleasing results of her experiments in free verse, a form rarely attempted by Canadian poets. Isabel Ecclestone (MacPherson) Mackay (1875-1928), whose name will be more familiar to some readers as a novelist than as a poet, and who won prizes for dramatic composition, wrote three volumes of verse, one of which, *The Shining Ship* (1918), contains excellent verse for children.

All the minor poets thus far considered in this discussion, except in the special respects indicated in passing, wrote on the same themes and in the same forms as the major poets. The difference between the major and minor groups is not in the kind of subject matter chosen or the artistic mould into which it is cast, but in the degree of excellence attained in the use of similar subject matter expressed in traditional forms. This is worth emphasizing as we turn from these poets to one whose poetic output is quite apart from the main current of Canadian verse.

Thomas Robert Edward MacInnes (1867-........) was born at Dresden, Ontario, of Scottish and Spanish stock, son of the late Honorable T. R. MacInnes, a doctor who was first a Member of Parliament, then a Senator, and finally a Lieutenant-Governor of British Columbia. The poet graduated in Arts from the University of Toronto in 1889, and was called to the Bar in 1893. During the years 1896 to 1910 he held different government appointments that brought him into contact with various parts of the Canadian Northwest, especially British Columbia and Yukon. He also drew up important legislation, including the Canadian Immigration Act. As a result of travel in China he is well informed on Oriental matters, and has written a prose work entitled *The Testament of the Ancient One,* on the subject of Chinese philosophy. He lives at Ottawa.

MacInnes's poetry falls into two periods, a romantic and a reflective. His first volume, twice reprinted, each time with a new title and a few additional poems, contains fantastic material reminiscent of Celtic and Scandinavian folk-story, of popular romance in general, and of Oriental romance in particular, the contact with the latter being either direct, or indirect through Thomas Moore. This fantastic material is, in the main, clothed in an atmosphere of horror after the manner of Poe. Poems that approach ordinary human experience are less vivid in setting and are touched by romantic love or by the grim romantic tragedy of pioneer life. In some of the romantic poems, an elusive symbolism, probably suggested by the allegorical element in Moore's oriental romance, and a trace of Oriental mysticism, mediated through Moore, Emerson, and Whitman, foreshadow the philosophical aspect of the second period, inaugurated with *Rhymes of a Rounder* (1913). In this volume and in subsequent poems, very much in the spirit of Omar Khayyam and François Villon but with more optimism, MacInnes, rejecting reformers, recognizing the virtues of courage, cleanliness, and charity, and facing all the mystery and the cruel facts of life, expresses, in elaborate French lyric forms suitably modified, satisfaction with the care-free, sensuous enjoyment of life, one day at a time. It is evident from these remarks that his philosophy of life runs counter to that usually accepted by Canadians, and as a result his artistic worth has been under-estimated, especially by those who cannot dissociate their aesthetic judgments from their opinions as to the soundness or unsoundness of the ideas embodied in a work of art. In both fantastic romance and Epicurean philosophy MacInnes holds a unique position in Canadian poetry.

Another figure who stands strikingly apart in the field of Canadian verse is Robert W. Service (1876-........), who was born at Preston, Lancashire, England. The family having moved to Scotland when Robert was six years old, he was educated at Hillhead high school, Glasgow, and at the University of Glasgow. After a brief tenure of a bank position in Glasgow, he came to Canada, made his way westward from city to city, and for five years travelled back and forth along the Pacific coast, engaging in various kinds of work, and residing temporarily in every city of importance as far south as Mexico. Later, as a clerk in the Canadian Bank of Commerce, he was stationed successively at Victoria, Vancouver, and Kamloops, in British Columbia, and at Whitehorse in the Yukon. During the second of the Balkan wars of 1912-3 and during the Great War he was war correspondent for the Toronto *Star,* and during two years of the Great War he drove an ambulance in a medical division. He has remained in Europe, and lives chiefly in Paris, France.

His work resembles that of Kipling, his avowed favourite author, in close observation of the "primal facts of life" and in the vivid, incisive diction in which he expresses his observations. Unlike his master, except in the few early poems that artistically reflect the spirit of the North, he rarely rises to the level of poetry, and that for two reasons. To his material, often sordidly and brutally realistic, he does not apply the principle of selection, which is necessary to produce good realistic or even naturalistic prose fiction, still more so to produce good poetry. Again, because of his fatal facility in popular metres and his lack of artistic conscience, he rarely attains formal excellence. His verse, the appeal of which lies in the broad human sympathy and the sense of reality that characterize his material and in the irresistible sweep of his unpolished rhythms, records a phase of life not typically but only transiently and accidentally

Canadian. The transitoriness of the kind of life that Service depicted accounts in the main for the fact that, though he had numerous imitators, of whom the most significant was Robert J. C. Stead, he has had no permanent following. To command attention, verse dealing with typical human conditions must have good form.

CHAPTER 29

POETS SINCE SERVICE

In this chapter we shall not attempt to arrange poets in
any order of merit. In most cases their work is still in-
complete; moreover, the perspective of time is needed to
evaluate judicially what they have already accomplished.
Again, the number of writers of verse is so great that it will
be impossible to mention all, even by name. The best that
can be done is to discuss the most significant of our younger
poets, and especially to bring out aspects of their art that
may not hitherto have received adequate critical recognition.

Norah Mary Holland (1876-1925), whose mother was
a first cousin of William Butler Yeats, and whose father
also inherited a poetic strain in his Irish blood, was born
at Collingwood, Ontario, and was educated at Port Dover
and Parkdale (Toronto) collegiate institutes. She became
a resident of Toronto in 1889. In 1904 she made a walking tour of the south and west of Ireland and of a considerable portion of England, the results of which are clearly
evident in her poems. After working for eight years with the

Dominion Press Clipping Bureau, she joined the staff of the Toronto *Daily News*.

Her essentially lyric genius so regularly found expression in light metres abounding in trisyllabic feet that there is little variety in her rhythmic patterns. Her poems in dialogue are far more lyric than dramatic. A pronounced vein of Celtic mysticism, chiefly concerned with the spiritual unseen lurking immediately behind the seen, and a strong tendency to the lyric of racial reminiscence, make her poems more Irish than Canadian.

Mrs. Amelia Beers (Warnock) Garvin, better known by her pen name, Katherine Hale (her mother's Christian name), was born at Galt, Ontario, of Scottish and American parentage. She supplemented the education received at Galt and at "Glen Mawr", a private school in Toronto, by study in New York and in Europe, with special attention to singing. The quality of her articles on Wagnerian opera, contributed from New York to the Toronto *Mail and Empire*, secured her appointment as Editor of Contemporary Literature with that paper, a position which she held until her marriage in 1912 to John W. Garvin, editor of several volumes of Canadian literature. Her editorial work was conducted under the pen name previously mentioned. Since her marriage her prose and verse have continued to appear in leading magazines. As early as 1908 she lectured in London, England, and elsewhere, on Canadian literature. She has continued and developed this kind of work, with the result that her lecture-recitals now

[233]

include folk-songs as well as literary readings. She has lectured widely in the United States and in Canada, largely under the auspices of outstanding clubs and associations.

Her prose work includes literary and musical criticism of high quality, successful short stories, and vividly colourful descriptive sketches of Canadian houses and cities of romance. In verse she has achieved distinction in various ways. Her descriptive poems display felicitous audacity in images and figures of speech and, because of her musical training, a special gift of interpreting colour in terms of music. Proof of her lyric excellence is the fact that several of her poems have been set to music, and sung by vocal artists of world fame. In the dramatic lyric, because of her power of imaginative sympathy, she has done even better work than in the lyric of personal emotion.

Marjorie Lowery Christie Pickthall (1883-1922), niece of the English author Marmaduke Pickthall, was born in London, England, and was educated at the Bishop Strachan School, Toronto, whither she came with her parents in 1890. When the war broke out, she was visiting relatives in England, and became interested in grey knitting and other work for the soldiers. Later she lived at Victoria, British Columbia.

From early childhood she practised writing, and was interested also in music and painting. Her work began to attract notice while she was still in her teens. In the short story, the poetic drama, and the novel her distinctive merits are vividness of setting and effectiveness of dramatic situation.

[234]

In the first two literary types she achieved also mastery of form, but in the novel she did not fully attain logical sequence of plot or consistency of characterization. Her genius was essentially lyric, and though her lyric powers increased as she continued to write, from the beginning her diction was felicitous from the standpoint of both imagery and verbal music. In the poetry of her first productive decade, because of her pagan love of classic myths, her interest in the unseen causes her to people with mermaids, nixies, sprites, and fauns the imagined world that she creates from her experience of Canadian nature. In the remaining period of her creative life, her treatment of the occult, of high spiritual ideals, and of deep emotional experiences is inspired largely by biblical and ecclesiastical history and legend, with the result that she has been compared to Christina Rossetti. Whether her poetic themes are pagan or Christian, her musical language and her beautiful, and usually Canadian, imagery rank her high among the women poets of Canada, some critics, indeed, conceding her first place, and all admitting her right to be included with Isabella Valancy Crawford and Emily Pauline Johnson in the trio of our best female poets.

John McCrae (1872-1918), though older than Service, belongs to the post-Service period as far as his poetry is concerned. He was born at Guelph, Ontario. At the early age of fourteen he joined the Guelph Highland Cadets, from which he later transferred to the artillery. He entered the University of Toronto in his sixteenth year with a scholarship for general proficiency, and graduated in Arts with honours in natural science in 1894, and in Medicine with a gold medal and a scholarship in 1898. In his subsequent medical study, practice, and teaching he was identified with different hospitals and universities; after 1900 chiefly with the Royal Victoria Hospital, Montreal, and the Medical School of McGill University. He served with the artillery during part of the Boer war and as Chief in Medicine in the McGill Unit for two years during the Great War. He died in France just after his appointment as Consulting Physician to the British Armies in the Field.

From his university days to the end, his one poetic theme was death, the tragic inevitability of which was deeply impressed on his sympathetic and refined nature by his experiences as a physician and by his historical and actual knowledge of war. He felt especially the tragedy in the death of those who die in the midst of a life work which they are pursuing with joyful zest. Some of his best poems make the dead anxious that the living shall continue the uncompleted task. McCrae was a very conscientious craftsman, and the relatively few poems that constitute his single posthumously published volume have a finish that ranks them high as specimens of Canadian poetic art.

Robert Winkworth Norwood (1874-........), collaterally of the same stock as Oliver Wendell Holmes, was born in Christ Church rectory, New Ross, Lunenburg County, Nova Scotia. Later, the family moved to the fishing village of Seaforth, Halifax County, on the south shore of Nova

Scotia, a fact to be remembered when reading *Bill Boram*. The poet had a varied academic career — one year at Coaticook Academy, Quebec, two years at the University of Bishop's College, Lennoxville, Quebec, five years at the University of King's College, Windsor, Nova Scotia, while Roberts was teaching English literature there, and two years at Columbia University as a graduate student in Philosophy. The University of King's College conferred on him the honorary degree of Doctor of Civil Law in 1921 and Acadia University the honorary degree of Doctor of Literature in 1924. He was ordained deacon in 1897, the year of his graduation in Arts from King's, and priest in 1898. He has held pastoral charges at Neils Harbour, Hubbards, Bridgewater, and Springhill, in Nova Scotia, at Trinity Church, Montreal, at Cronyn Memorial Church, London, Ontario, at Memorial Church of St. Paul, Overbrook, Philadelphia, and at St. Bartholomew's, New York, his present charge.

Norwood has published four volumes containing chiefly lyric poems, one long narrative poem, two poetic dramas, and four volumes of prose. Whether he is writing in prose or in verse, his ultimate purpose is to interpret the universe in terms of Divine Love. Characters in whose lives he finds Divine Love exemplified are his favourite poetic subject; hence his supreme interest in the personality of Jesus as the perfect incarnation of Divine Love.

Wilson MacDonald (1880-........) was born at Cheapside, Ontario. His father, a native of Scotland, was a merchant and Baptist preacher, and his mother was the daughter of a Baptist minister. The poet was educated at the schools of Port Dover, at Woodstock College, and at the University of Toronto. In 1902 he worked his way on a cattle-boat to England, where he spent several months. On his return to Canada he worked for a while as a banker, and then spent a year travelling in the United States. He has visited twenty states of the Union, has sailed the Labrador Coast and the Pacific Coast from Mexico almost to Alaska, and has lived in every province of Canada except Prince Edward Island. In Ontario and British Columbia in particular, he has experienced life in the wilds. In addition to writing poetry, he has invented patentable devices and achieved some success as illuminator and musician. At present he lives in Toronto and devotes himself to writing poetry except when on tour giving lecture-recitals of his own poetry.

MacDonald early displayed the desire and the determination to become a poet, in which he was encouraged at home, at school, and at college. As a result he has reached a high level of attainment. His early work manifested romantic tendencies — a preference of natural to ordered beauty, an inclination to attach more importance to subject matter than to form, humanitarian sentiment, and Oriental mysticism. This last characteristic, and not egotism, is the explanation of his use of the first personal pronoun somewhat in the manner of Emerson (as in "Brahma") and especially in the manner of Whitman (as in "Song of Myself"). His poetry records varied experiences, but supremely his quest for Beauty, which unifies life and gives to it its highest fruition in brotherhood and love.

Alexander M. Stephen (1882-........) was born near Hanover, Ontario, of Scottish ancestry. His mother was a descendant of poets, and his father, a public-school principal, was a relative of Sir Leslie Stephen, the eminent English biographer and critic. The poet was educated at the public schools of Hanover and at Walkerton Collegiate Institute. He went to British Columbia in his early teens and has spent the greater part of his life in the Canadian West. Soon after going to British Columbia, he was articled to a law firm, but was unable to resist the lure to adventure of the Klondike rush. He has experienced many activities of pioneer life — prospecting and mining, homesteading, ranching, and teaching school in remote districts. His wanderings have taken him as far south as Mexico. Having studied architecture and obtained the degree of Bachelor of Science from Chicago University, he became a professional architect, a phase of his experience that terminated when the Great War took him overseas. After his return to Vancouver he spent some time first in teaching school and then in the practice of engineering. Now he is associate editor of the *Western Tribune,* and his work on this paper and his purely literary activities occupy all of his working time. He is keenly interested also in community welfare.

Stephen has edited two volumes of Canadian verse and published two novels and two volumes of poetry. That he is essentially a poet is shown by the romantic and poetic glamour of his prose fiction. The poems of his first volume, *The Rosary of Pan* (1923), though not always felicitous in metre and diction, revealed poetic genius. *The Land of Singing Waters* (1927) showed that, by careful attention to imagery and by assiduous practice of verse forms, even the most difficult, he had overcome his weaknesses. While there is a great variety of subject matter in his poetry, he is primarily a mystical poet with a message for mankind. He is a dreamer of dreams in which his deep and fervent imagination attains to cosmic vision, to the realization of "One Sublime Reality" that embraces all finite realities.

Edwin J. Pratt (1883-........), son of a Methodist minister, was born at Western Bay, an "outport" of Newfoundland. He thus spent his early days with the roar of the Atlantic and the tales of sailors ever sounding in his ears. His familiarity with the ocean was increased by a long period on a fishing-vessel off the Banks. He was educated at the Methodist College at St. John's, Newfoundland, and, from 1907 to 1911, at Victoria College, University of Toronto, where he now teaches English literature.

Newfoundland Verse (1923) contains material unsurpassed in Canadian literature in its descriptive, interpretive, and dramatic treatment of the relentless, unconquerable sea. *The Witches' Brew* (1926) is an intellectual *tour de force,* in which the author satirizes men and things with pointed cleverness and subtle humour. In *The Titans* (1926) the intellectual element is still present in the ingenious choice of words and in the manipulation of metre and rhyme, but the epic and dramatic qualities of the narrative in both poems make also a strong imaginative and emotional appeal. Late in 1926, Pratt lost his mother, whom, from the time that he left home in his early twenties, he had made a point of visiting every summer. His sorrow led him to meditate on life beyond the veil, and in 1927 he published the results of his meditation in an elaborate and noble ode entitled *The Iron Door*. In his latest work, *The Roosevelt and the Antinoe* (1930), based on an actual occurrence in January, 1926, he combined two things in which he had previously achieved success separately, namely, representation of the sea and epic narrative, and produced a highly meritorious poem, one that is likely to advance his rank among Canadian poets.

Bernard Freeman Trotter (1890-1917), a first cousin of Mary Josephine (Trotter) Benson (1887-........), was born at Toronto while his father, a Baptist minister of English descent, was a professor at McMaster University. The father became President of Acadia University, and the son consequently spent the impressionable years from five to fifteen at Wolfville, Nova Scotia, in the heart of the Land of Evangeline. He was educated at Horton Collegiate Academy, Wolfville, at Woodstock College, and, after a three years' residence in California for his health, at McMaster University, from which he graduated in 1915. During this senior year he drilled in the Canadian Officers' Training Corps. In December, 1916, after about nine months' training in England, he crossed to France. Within five months he was killed.

He began to write verse at the age of fourteen. From the first there were present in a marked degree qualities which improved as he continued to write, — delicate fancy, good imagery, and music resulting from native facility in metre, rhyme, assonance, and alliteration. His instinctive love of nature, intensified by his three years in California and by his outdoor college vacations, finds expression in nature poems with Wordsworthian touches of description and reflection. His later work foreshadows a turning from poetry that expresses enjoyment of the beauty and wonder of the world to poetry that deals, in a Tennysonian rather than in a Wordsworthian manner, with the problems of human life. The rich promise of his work in material and technique therefore suggests a parallel between the loss that Keats' death meant to English literature and the loss that Trotter's death meant to Canadian literature.

CHAPTER 30

WILLIAM HENRY DRUMMOND
(1854-1907)

Drummond has been reserved for study immediately before our consideration of French-Canadian literature because of his unique position as an interpreter of the French-Canadian people. This does not mean that no other Canadian writer has done literary work somewhat similar in kind. As a matter of fact, the collection of tales by Duncan Campbell Scott entitled *In the Village of Viger* (1896), which was published before the first volume of Drummond's verse appeared, and William McLennan's volume of tales entitled *In Old France and New* (1899), contain sympathetic representations of the humour and pathos of French-Canadian life, and Scott has written also a one-act play entitled *Pierre,* the title of which indicates the source of the material. But all of this work is written in prose and in the case of each author constitutes in quantity a minor portion of his work. In *The Little Admiral* (1924), a novel for boys, Jean McIlwraith wrote with the purpose of "instilling into young Canadians of British extraction more sympathy

[243]

for their fellow-countrymen, the French, than is usually displayed." Her purpose is similar to that of Drummond, but the style of this juvenile fiction is of necessity very different from that of Drummond's verse.

Mrs. S. Frances Harrison, in *Pine, Rose and Fleur-de-Lis* (1891), wrote of the French-Canadians sympathetically in verse some years before the publication of Drummond's first volume. But with all her sympathy we are conscious that it is an outsider telling outsiders about the French-Canadians. Frank Oliver Call (1878-........), by casting the *habitant* material of *Blue Homespun* (1925), tends to give the reader a similar impression of detached observation.

Drummond, on the other hand, makes the French-Canadians reveal themselves to us almost as if we were one with them. This dramatic vividness is largely due to the fact that, instead of employing dialect for purposes of ridicule, as it had hitherto been almost exclusively used in literature with French-Canadian characters, he employed it with sympathetic understanding, and made his characters talk much as they would if they were telling their experiences to English-speaking persons who do not understand French. For the distinctive aspects of his work Drummond was fitted by temperament and by the circumstances of his life.

The son of an officer in the Royal Irish Constabulary, he was born near Mohill, County Leitrim, Ireland. When he was two years old, the family moved to Tawley, a beautiful and romantic village, situated on a mountain overlooking the Bay of Donegal, where they lived for about seven years. Then, after a short visit to Mohill, they came to Canada, where the father soon died. Through the heroism of the mother, Drummond's education, begun at Tawley, was continued for a time at a private school. To relieve his mother's burden by contributing to the family budget, he learned telegraphy. As an operator at Bord-à-Plouffe he first came in contact with French-Canadian life. Later he continued his education at the High School, Montreal, at McGill University, and at Bishop's College, Lennoxville, Quebec, from which he graduated in medicine in 1884. After two years' practice each at Stornaway and Knowlton, he settled permanently in Montreal. For several years he was Professor of Medical Jurisprudence at McGill University. He died of cerebral haemorrhage while heroically fighting smallpox at the Cobalt mines, in which he was interested during the last two years of his life.

His poetry, in the production of which he was greatly encouraged by his wife, is largely a by-product of his experience as telegrapher, camper, and medical practitioner. His interpretation of Irish-Canadian life has not yet received adequate recognition, because it is overshadowed by his successful interpretation of French-Canadian types — the *habitant,* the *voyageur,* and the *coureur de bois.* We have already seen how the events of his life prepared him for this work. His temperament led to his success in two outstanding ways: he had a whole-hearted appreciation of nature and a sympathetic admiration of the simplicity of French-Canadian life. S. Weir Mitchell wrote of him:—

"With nature as with man at home, he loved
    The silent forest and the birches' flight
Down the white peril of the rapids' rush,
    And the cold glamour of your Northern night."

And Drummond addresses these lines to his readers:—

"Remember when these tales you read
    Of rude but honest "Canayen,"
That Joliet, La Verendrye,
    La Salle, Marquette, and Hennepin
Were all true "Canayen" themselves —
    And in their veins the same red stream:
The conquering blood of Normandie
    Flowed strong, and gave America
Coureurs de bois and *voyageurs*
    Whose trail extends from sea to sea!"

These two aspects of Drummond's temperament may be
shown in happy combination by quoting from his poems.
Here is his picture of French-Canadian home life in the
winter:—

"An' some cole winter night how I wish you can see us,
    W'en I smoke on de pipe, an' de ole woman sew
By de stove of T'ree Reever — ma wife's fader geev her
    On day we get marry, dat's long tam ago —

De boy an' de girl, dey was readin' it's lesson,
    De cat on de corner she's bite heem de pup,

[246]

Ole "Carleau" he's snorin' an' beeg stove is roarin'
So loud dat I'm scare purty soon she bus' up."

Isidore, the "feller" of Philomene, the oldest child, calls:—

"But nine o'clock strike, an' de chil'ren is sleepy,
Mese'f an' ole woman can't stay up no more,
So alone by de fire — 'cos dey say dey ain't tire —
We lef' Philomene an' de young Isidore."

"The Habitant's Summer" records the change from winter
to spring and summer:—

"O! who can blame de winter, never min' de hard he's
blowin'
'Cos w'en de tam is comin' for passin' on hees roun'
De firse t'ing he was doin' is start de sky a snowin'
An' mak' de nice w'ite blanket, for cover up de groun'.

* * * * *

Den you geev her leetle sunshine, w'en de snow go off
an' leave her
Let de sout'win' blow upon her, an' you see beeg changes
now
Wit' de steam arisin' from her jus' de sam' she got de
fever,
An' not many day is passin' w'en she's ready for de
plough."

* * * * *

Spring brings apple blossoms and trout, but the *habitant*
is too busy to go fishing:—

"For de mos' fine summer season don't las' too long,
   an' we know it,
So we're workin' ev'rybody, w'ile de sun is warm an'
   clear,
Dat's de tam for plant de barley, an' de Injun corn
   we sow it,
W'en de leaf upon de maple's jus' de size of squirrel's
   ear.

'Noder job is feexin' fences, if we don't be lak de las'
   year,
W'en de Durham bull he's pullin' nearly all de fence
   away,
An' dat sapree champion taureau let de cattle out de
   pasture
So dey're playin' on de devil wit' de oat an' wit' de
   hay."

Such minor vexations do not mar the happiness of the
habitant :—

"For dere's no place lak our own place, don't care de
   far you're goin'
Dat's w'at de whole worl's sayin', w'enever dey come
   here,
'Cos we got de fines' contree, an' de beeges' reever
   flowin'
An' le bon Dieu sen' de sunshine nearly twelve mont'
   ev'ry year."

These few extracts are sufficient to reveal the qualities of temperament that fitted Drummond for his great achievement and to suggest a number of his distinguishing characteristics. Having learned by long association with French-Canadians to admire and love them, and possessing a native appreciation of the simplicity of their lives and of their natural environment, Drummond characterized them with unrivalled picturesqueness, humour, pathos, and skill in dialect. To quote Mitchell again:—

"He made his own the thoughts of simple men,
    And with the touch that makes the world akin
A welcome guest of lonely cabin homes,
    Found, too, no heart he could not enter in.

The toil-worn doctor, women, children, men,
    The humble heroes of the lumber drives,
Love, laugh, or weep along his peopled verse,
    Blithe 'mid the pathos of their meagre lives.

While thus the poet-love interpreted,
    He left us pictures no one may forget —
Courteau, Batiste, Camille mon frère and best,
    The good brave curé, he of Calumette."

As a Canadian man of letters Drummond is of great significance in two ways. The importance of the two chief races of Canada understanding each other, and particularly of the English-speaking element understanding the French, is incalculable. In this practical way Drummond has rendered a service that cannot easily be over-estimated. From the artistic point of view, his unparalleled sympathetic and realistic interpretation of a very important element in Canadian life gives him a unique place among the poets of Canada, of the Empire, and even of the world.

CHAPTER 31

FRENCH-CANADIAN LITERATURE

The preceding discussion has suggested how important it is for the British and French elements of the Canadian population to understand each other. One of the best ways of accomplishing this desirable result would be for each to read the literature of the other in the tongue in which it is written. Unfortunately, however, the number of bilingual Canadian citizens is comparatively small, and such mutual appreciation of literary achievement as is possible for the majority must be attained in other ways. As far as English-speaking Canadians are concerned, it is possible to read literature such as that discussed in the preceding section, to read in translation such illuminating works as Rivard's *Chez Nous* and Hémon's *Maria Chapdelaine,* and to read an historical account of French-Canadian literature, either in summary outline, as we must present it here, or in more detail, as found in MacMechan and Pierce.

The history of French-Canadian literature naturally begins in Quebec, For nearly one hundred years after Canada was finally ceded to the English, there was almost nothing written of significance as French-Canadian literature. There was not a little literary activity in the way of conducting short-lived newspapers and magazines, but this was carried on not by citizens but by Frenchmen of France whose residence in Canada was rather accidental than otherwise. One exception is Michel Bibaud (1782-1857), the first French historian of Canada, and author of the first volume of verse by a born Canadian. His verse, largely satiric of the natural frailties of the French-Canadian population, would tend not so much to stimulate other writers as to laugh out of existence, after the manner of comedy, the very qualities that furnish at least part of the material for literature. His history, because it took the side of the English against the French, was unpopular with his own people, and so of no influence in creating literature based on local patriotism.

Between the years 1845 and 1852, however, François Xavier Garneau (1809-66), by writing a *Histoire du Canada* in which he held a brief for his countrymen and showed that their defeat was as glorious as a victory, created a local patriotism that brought into being in Quebec between the years 1860 and 1870 the first school of French-Canadian literature. By revealing to his people their past, and arousing their racial pride, Garneau founded a school of historians and poets.

In Quebec in 1860 there was a small bookstore kept by three brothers named Crémazie, one of whom, Octave, possessed poetic genius. In this bookstore Garneau the historian and other *intelligentsia* of Quebec came in contact with each other. With the French instinct for organization in aesthetic matters, they established a magazine, *Les Soirées Canadiennes,* as a medium through which "to relate the delightful tales of the people before they have forgotten them."

The racial pride aroused by Garneau's history was greatly augmented for this literary group by the coming to Quebec, during the Crimean war, of the French frigate *Capricieuse,* flying the French flag. Not since the conquest had the French flag been displayed in French Canada, and although it was the tricolour of the republic instead of the old flag of Catholic France, yet it symbolized the great achievements of the French race and founded a Napoleonic legend in French Canada. The literary result was in general not a little verse and in particular the awakening of Crémazie's genius.

As the result of what the commercial world of his time called a forgery, Crémazie left Canada in 1862 and lived the rest of his life in France under an assumed name. There he, a devotee of the cult of Napoleon, sustained the horrors of the siege of Paris and was an eye-witness of the downfall of Napoleon II. In prose Crémazie reveals excellent literary taste and a clear, forceful style illuminated by flashes of characteristically French wit. His verse is of small quantity but high quality. He wrote a very successful atmosphere poem, *Promenade de Trois Morts,* after the school of Poe. Another poem, *Le Drapeau de Carillon,* the sentiment of

[253]

which is perhaps unconsciously false, expresses the regret of the *habitant* at being cast off by the French and being left to the mercy of the British. This poem appeals to French-Canadians, and Hébert has rendered the conception in bronze in the monument to the poet in Saint Louis Square, Montreal. French-Canadians can enjoy equally well another poem that appeals also to English-speaking Canadians, one of the finest poems about one of the most beautiful aspects of Canadian scenery, the Thousand Isles. The most important characteristic of Crémazie for Canadians as a whole is his enthusiastic love of the Canadian scene, the beauties of which are transcribed from the memories of an exile.

Another poet of the Quebec school, who showed more anti-English feeling than Crémazie, was Pamphile Le May (1837-1918), noted for his translation into French of Longfellow's *Evangeline,* and for his successful pictures of the rustic activities of the French-Canadians. His success as a poet of his people is at once the gratification of his own literary ambition and his chief significance.

Greatest of the Quebec school of French-Canadian literature, was an avowed disciple of Crémazie, Louis Fréchette (1839-1903). Like his master, he found in the scenery and history of Canada his chief sources of poetic inspiration. Unable, like many another Canadian man of letters, to obtain a satisfactory livelihood in Canada, he spent a number of years in the United States, where he fought a duel with a Prussian during the Franco-Prussian war. After his return to Quebec in 1871, he practised law and for a number of years was in politics. His wife was a sister of William Dean Howells, noted American man of letters. Besides a vast mass of journalistic work, he wrote poetry, drama, history, and prose satire. His early volumes of verse, like those of his master Crémazie, show his enthusiasm for French family life and for the scenery of the St. Lawrence. His second volume won him a Montyon prize from the French Academy, and in 1884 he was crowned by that august body. In his chief work in verse, *Legende d'un Peuple,* he aims to be the Garneau of poetry. As is to be expected, he is even more partial than Garneau to his own people. Nevertheless, he presents with considerable epic garndeur the story of the French in Canada. His prose includes character sketches of some of the inconsistent types that are the natural product of a provincial environment. His dramas *Montcalm* and *Papineau* challenge our attention not so much as works of art as indications of his interest in Canadian history. He is significant, as the national poet of the French-Canadians, in finding his themes at home, in giving expression to the national legend, in revealing to the French-Canadians their country and themselves, and in doing this with such art as to win the approval of the French Academy.

Other literary men belonging to the Quebec school are Abbé H. R. Casgrain (1831-1904), whose *Pèlerinage au Pays D'Evangeline* tells sympathetically and eloquently the story of the Acadians; Gérin-Lajoie (1824-82), whose *Un Canadien Errant* is a truly national poem, based on the exile of French-Canadians as a result of the rebellion of 1837; Philippe Aubert de Gaspé (1786-1871), whose romance *Les Anciens Canadiens,* of little merit as a work of fiction, is a veritable mine of information about the French Régime (It has been translated into English by Roberts).

Montreal, also, has been the home of a school of French-Canadian literature. As in the case of the Quebec school, the French genius for organization manifested itself, even before the founding of the school. In the early nineties of the last century, a number of literary young Frenchmen in Montreal formed a Society, one of the first definite results of which was the publication of two literary journals. The first number of one of these, the *Echo des Jeunes,* shows that the new Society is opposed to the Quebec school in ideals and aims. The Quebec school was imitative of Victor Hugo and Lamartine, representative authors of the Romantic Movement in Old France. The Montreal school, a school of youth in revolt against the old, displayed considerable independence, but so far as it accepted models it turned to de Heredia and Leconte de Lisle, representative of the French *Parnassiens,* whose distinctive characteristic is their reaction against the excesses of the Romanticists, some of whom the Quebec school had taken as their masters. The *Parnassiens,* while recognizing the rich variety of subject matter among the Romanticists, resented their lack of form and their abandon, and set themselves to the task of restoring artistic restraint and excellence of form. Apart from their *penchant* for description of tropical scenery they do just what we should expect; they favour classical subjects and write in exquisitely finished style. With such models, the Montreal school was bound to produce work different from that of the Quebec school.

By 1915 a group of these Montreal young men had decided to form themselves into a school of literature, that is, they made provision for mutual criticism of their own work and for the evaluation and improvement of the work of other literary aspirants who wished to join the Society. The members, young university graduates, met on Friday evenings in the Château de Ramezay. Eventually Fréchette, of the Quebec group, became honorary president of the Montreal organization. In 1900 the group published an anthology, *Soirées du Château de Ramezay,* and soon after, the school as an institution came to an end. The anthology brought forward two young men worthy of note.

One of these was Émile Nelligan (1882-........), son of an Irish father and a French mother. Constitutionally melancholy, Nelligan became insane at the age of nineteen. His verse shows a characteristic difference between the Quebec and Montreal schools. The writers of the former school, as was natural with their romantic leanings, found their subject matter chiefly in Canada and the Church. The Montreal poets as a rule avoided these themes. Nelligan's poetry has very little to do with Canada. His poems contain no echoes of Canadian history, no pictures of Canadian landscape, little or no internal evidence that they were written in Canada. Nor does he write of France, or of the Napoleonic legend, which fascinated some of the Quebec poets. His poetry, characterized by richly musical verse and finished formal excellence, is in the main subjective, with fantastic imagery and a morbid strangeness that reminds one of Poe. So far as he made the Church the subject of his verse, he was attracted by the poetry of her ritual and the sensuous beauty of her accessories. His sadness, the strangeness of his imagery, the music of his verse, and the tragedy of his fate, give him a unique place in the history of Canadian literature.

The second man of outstanding talent represented in the anthology of the Montreal school was Albert Lozeau (1875-1924). He too was a sufferer, long an invalid, having been smitten in his boyhood with a disease that confined him to his bed. The parallel with Heine, the German poet, arrests attention. Before his sickness he had taken a commercial course, so that he knew nothing of Latin or of French literature. While he was bed-ridden he made his acquaintance with several of the great masters of French literature. Though naturally akin to the Montreal school, he was, on account of his affliction, unable to participate in their literary evenings. This probably made him more independent of the masters to whom the Montreal school turned, in so far as they accepted models at all, and tended toward the development of his talent along more original lines.

His first volume, *L'Ame Solitaire,* contains his most important work. The striking thing about his poetry is its cheerful spirit. In it there is no tendency to morbidity,

[258]

to pessimism, to self-pity. Surprising, too, is the fact that he writes successful love poetry, something very rare in Canadian poets, English or French. Lozeau, bed-ridden in a city room, differs from the other members of the Montreal school in that he makes Canadian nature a theme of his poetry. Like Roberts, Lampman, and D. C. Scott, he follows the course of the seasons through the year, and, like a true Canadian, delights equally in the cold of winter and the heat of summer. His poetry of the seasons could have been written only by a Canadian poet about the Canadian year. Another characteristic of Lozeau is his intense love of music and the eloquence with which he has written of it in his poetry. He has written also poems of reflection, in which he expresses his simple philosophy of life, a stoical, mild pessimism.

Not directly connected with the Montreal school of literature, but belonging in spirit to the literary movement which it inaugurated, is Paul Morin (1889-........), distinctive among Canadian men of letters for his cultural training acquired by travel and study. His scholastic standing may be suggested by mentioning the fact that his doctorial thesis at the University of Paris, a study in the sources of Longfellow's poems, required a knowledge of practically every literary language of Europe. At the age of twenty-two he had not only completed this training but also published his first volume of poetry, in Paris. Like the founders of the Montreal school, he is a *Parnassien*. His work is therefore marked by perfection of form and by skilful description of picturesque foreign scenery, and his first book may be ranked artistically as the best volume of French verse written by a Canadian. With his second volume in 1923 he won a prize of two thousand dollars from the Quebec Government, a government that deserves emulation for the way in which it encourages the production of works of art. Whether or not in the future Morin develops, in addition to his pictorial power, the power of reflection, he is sure, on the basis of his present achievement, of a permanent place in the literature of Canada.

The writers of the Montreal school, with their greater learning, superior critical faculty, and primary interest in good form, have undoubtedly achieved a greater artistic success than their brethren of the Quebec school, but their work, with the exception of that of Lozeau, might have been written almost anywhere, whereas the writers of the Quebec school have a special appeal to Canadian readers because of their literary expression of their love of the natural beauty of their own Canadian home.

CHAPTER 32

CONCLUSION

In the preceding discussions we have considered the most significant work of the outstanding Canadian authors in the various forms of literature, and from our survey several conclusions may be drawn. One is that the highest artistic level in Canadian literature has been reached in poetry, and that the best Canadian poetry has been written by the poets of the "Group of the Sixties", Campbell, Pauline Johnson, Roberts, Carman, Lampman, and the Scotts. How many of the younger poets have produced or give promise of producing work of equal artistic worth, cannot be so easily decided. It may safely be said, however, that, taking into account the poetic quality of the work of the younger men and women already considered and of various others, such as Lloyd Roberts, Louise Morey Bowman, and Marian Osborne, the prospect for Canadian poetry is bright.

The Canadian novel has been almost wholly restricted to the realm of romance, and especially to the historical region of that realm. Within these boundaries there has been a considerable amount of satisfactory achievement. Very few

Canadian novelists have persistently endeavoured to extend the domain of the novel into the realm of realism, in which the greatest novelists of other lands have done their greatest work. A few novelists have produced incidentally one or two genuinely realistic novels, but our only consistent realist, and by the same token the most likely to be ranked as our greatest novelist, is F. P. Grove. The future of the Canadian novel depends on whether we remain a race of romanticists or become mature enough in taste to be realists, at least part of the time.

Canadian drama has been limited even more than the Canadian novel by the romantic taste of the Canadian public. However romantic a subject may be in plot or in setting, the form of the novel is sufficiently flexible to give it adequate expression, but the limitations of the stage render impossible the dramatic treatment of many a romantic subject. With a limited number of romantic subjects that can be presented in the theatre and with no demand for realistic drama, the production of plays for the Canadian stage has been very meagre. Merrill Denison has made a forceful attempt in the direction of realism in Canadian drama, and there is some hope in the Little Theatre movement and, in association therewith, the increasing attention paid to the one-act play.

The Canadian short story also has been limited by the romantic taste of Canadian readers, but somewhat less so than the novel and very much less so than the drama. Depending on the intrinsic interest of their romantic mat-

ial, Canadian writers of the short story may not at all
mes have been sufficiently careful in technique, with a
nsequent further detrimental effect on the artistic quality
the Canadian short story. At present, more attention
being paid to realistic treatment in short fiction, and the
dvance in technical proficiency is shown by the recognition
r excellence that Canadian short stories receive in con-
mporary critical evaluations of current short fiction.

The present status and future prospect of non-fictional
anadian prose are very satisfactory. Biography and history
prove as Canadian biographers and historians become cap-
le of supplementing factual accuracy and philosophical
sight with imaginative power. Our formal essayists com-
re favourably in number and quality with those of other
untries, and the number of our good literary essayists will
come larger with increasing material prosperity and ad-
ncing culture. Development in culture will also increase
e quantity and improve the quality of our humorous lit-
ature. In the field of descriptive or local-colour writing,
r contemporary artists maintain the high standard set in
e early days by such writers as Mrs. Moodie and Mrs.
meson.

After viewing this varied achievement of Canadian men
d women of letters, one naturally asks if Canadian lit-
ature as a whole reflects a spirit that may be called the
irit of Canadian literature. Canada is a young country,
d in general the spirit of its literature is the spirit of
uth. Youth is characterized by simplicity, sincerity, eager-

[263]

ness, romanticism, idealism, optimism, courage, and the spi
of adventure, and all of these qualities are found in Ca
adian literature. The attitude of youth toward conventi
is often inconsistent, and this is true also of the spirit of Ca
adian literature. Our writers on the whole have been ve
careful to treat conventional subjects in conventional forn
But though very few have experimented with new them
or new forms, not a few have been rather no
chalantly unconventional in their handling of conventior
forms, as witness the liberties taken with the form of o
of the most technically formal of lyrics, the sonnet. Tl
is very much in the spirit displayed by youth at that sta
of its development in which it slights, rather than resis
convention. With approaching puberty we may expect i
creasing experimentation in subject matter and in for.

More important than whether Canadian literature has
distinctively characteristic spirit is, for reasons that will
given later, whether it reflects a consciousness of nationali
Our Dominion, in common with other countries, has tv
fundamental bases of national patriotism, love of the la
itself and pride in the achievements of the people. Wi
regard to the former, in the literature of no other count
does the description of nature smack more of the soil of t
region that produced it than it does in Canadian literatu
Poets like Roberts, Lampman, Duncan Campbell Scott, a
Lozeau, in their descriptive verse vividly present the vario
aspects of nature throughout the year, and it is distinctive
a Canadian year of Canadian nature. Our local-colo

[264]

writers as well as some of our poets write pictorial and atmospheric descriptions of particular regions the conditions in
which could not exist outside of Canada, and they do it in
a manner that makes us feel that these regions are a part of
our country and therefore not alien to our interest. In literature the prairies, as represented by Grove, for example,
do not belong to the prairie provinces, but to all of Canada,
and the same is true of literary representations of the Atlantic
region, the St. Lawrence waterways, the Laurentians, the
Niagara district, the Great Lakes, the Rocky Mountains,
and the Pacific coast. Canadian literature expresses what
may be called a national consciousness of the rich and varied
natural beauty of Canada.

With regard to literature of national patriotism based
on pride in the achievements of the Canadian people, because
Canada is a young nation, we have, in addition to verse com-
memorating noble deeds of the past, verse that arouses
patriotic fervour through its vision of possible future attainment. Though such patriotic literature, like literature that
expresses love of the soil, may be regional rather than
national in its appeal, it is nevertheless true that the note
of pride in Canadian accomplishment as sounded in Canadian literature as a whole, elicits an emotional response
broad enough in its appeal to be of national significance.

Why is the question of national consciousness in Canadian literature of such great importance? For several
weighty reasons. First, national consciousness is a great
stimulus to the creation of literature. Great literature

[265]

is produced in periods when peoples are profoundly moved, and for such creative activity due to public emotion there has been no more fruitful source than national sentiment aroused by concentration on a national cause. This is amply shown by reference to the history of Old-World literatures, and it would be of great interest to know to what extent the work of the "Group of the Sixties" is the result of the effect upon them during their most impressionable years of the accomplished fact of Confederation. Further, literature that is the product of national consciousness stimulates in turn that which produced it, and so the good results of national consciousness are cumulative.

There is another and even weightier reason why the question of national consciousness in Canadian literature is important. It is vitally essential to the future welfare of Canada that Canadians, whatever language they speak, should feel that they are one people. Obviously this sense of unity cannot come from the possession of a common tongue; we are and must remain a bilingual people. Obviously, also, it cannot come from the possession of a common religion. Undue attention to race, language, and religion would, because of basic differences, tend to disruption rather than unity. National consciousness, on the other hand, is a sure and safe basis for the sentiment of national unity. Canadians, whether they speak English or French, may be one in their love of Canadian soil and in their pride in Canadian achievement.

[266]

Conclusion

The two other means of fostering such love and pride are Canadian history and Canadian literature, neither of which has been adequately used for the purpose. Our concern here is primarily with Canadian literature, the influence of which in this way is twofold. First, so far as it expresses national consciousness it tends to develop national sentiment in its readers. Furthermore, Canadian literature itself, whether it reflects national sentiment or not, is one of the most worthy sources of that pride in national achievement which is one of the strongest bases of national sentiment. And the wider the knowledge of Canadian literature on which such pride in achievement rests, the more unifying is the sentiment to which it gives life and growth. The more English-speaking Canadians can appreciate the literature written by their French-Canadian brothers, the more will they forget the things that tend to put asunder, and the more will they remember the importance of national unity, the ideal of which was well expressed by one of our earliest poets to catch its vision and feel its glow:

"One voice, one people, one in heart,
And soul, and feeling, and desire."

A SYLLABUS FOR THE STUDY OF CANADIAN LITERATURE

NOTE 1.—So far as is practicable, and with reasonable attention to chronological order, this book takes up first writing that is the record of actual experience, such as journals, memoirs, travels, biography, and history, because it is much easier for the general reader to appreciate material of its kind than it is for him to appreciate imaginative literature, especially the higher types. The types of imaginative literature are approached as much as possible in the order of their difficulty, the study of narrative fiction, drama, and poetry coming in the later chapters. This order should enable the student to discern the relation between Canadian life and Canadian literature, to devlop a discriminating apperciation of the forms of Canadian literature, and to ascertain whether there is a Canadian national sentiment of which Canadian men and women of letters are the voice.

NOTE 2.—Since the appropriate sections of this volume correspond exactly in number and title with the following chapters, they have not been otherwise designated in the syllabus. Anthologies and handbooks are referred to briefly by the names of the editors or authors. The anthologies referred to (other than complete volumes) are: Broadus, *A Book of Canadian Prose and Verse* (Macmillan); Garvin, *Canadian Poets*, 1926 edition (McClelland and Stewart). The handbooks to which reference is made are: Baker, *A History of English-Canadian Literature to the Confederation* (Harvard University Press), invaluable for the period covered; Pierce, *An Outline of Canadian Literature* (Ryerson Press), the most complete handbook of Canadian literature, English and French; MacMechan, *Headwaters of Canadian Literature* (McClelland and Stewart), containing a valuable sketch of French-Canadian literature and very judicious estimates of the work of all writers discussed; Logan and French, *Highways of Canadian Literature* (McClelland and Stewart), in which Logan's evaluations of the writers examined are sometimes highly personal.

CHAPTER 1: Introduction. See also Chapter I of Baker and of Pierce.

CHAPTER 2: Puritan Literature;—Henry Alline, *Life and Journal,* especially pp. 3–6, 9–11, 20–4, 31–46, and *Hymns,* Bk. I, Nos. 57, 59, Bk. II, No. 50, Bk. III, Nos. 65, 90, Bk. IV, No. 20, Bk. V, No. 99. See also Baker, Chapter II.

CHAPTER 3: Loyalist Literature;—Broadus, pp. 3–7. See also Baker, Chapter III, and M. C. Tyler, *Literary History of the American Revolution* (Putnam), the chapters on Inglis, Stansbury, and Odell.

[269]

CHAPTER 4: Scottish Literature;—Broadus, pp. 27–32. See also W. R. Mackenzie, *Ballads and Sea Songs from Nova Scotia* (Harvard University Press); Baker, Chapter XVII; Logan, Chapter I.

CHAPTER 5: Joseph Howe;—Broadus, pp. 24–7, 323–42. See also *Speeches and Public Letters* and *Poems and Essays;* Baker, Chapter V; Pierce, pp. 129–30; Mac-Mechan, pp. 44–6; Logan, Chapter III; biographies of Howe by Grant and Longley.

CHAPTER 6: Thomas Chandler Haliburton;—Broadus pp. 105–8, 186–210; *The Clock Maker, The Attaché,* and *The Old Judge* contain excellent material. See also Baker, Chapter VI; Pierce, pp. 161–4, MacMechan, pp. 36–44; Logan, Chapter IV; biographies by Logan and Chittick.

CHAPTER 7: Travels, Exploration, and Memoirs;—Broadus, pp. 18–20, 160–86, 210–22; if convenient, Mackenzie's *Voyages,* Henry's *Travels and Adventures,* Mrs. Moodie's *Roughing It . . .* (McClelland and Stewart) and Mrs. Jameson's *Winter Studies and Summer Rambles* (same). See also Baker, Chapter X, XIII; Pierce, pp. 156–7, 207–11; Logan, Chapter II.

CHAPTER 8: History and Biography;—Roberts, *History of Canada;* Michael Williams, *The Book of the High Romance* (Macmillan); F. P. Grove, *A Search for America* (Graphic). See also Baker, Chapter VIII; Pierce, Chapter X, XII; Logan, Chapter XXXI.

CHAPTER 9: Rise of the Canadian Historical Novel;— ᵒadus, pp. 148–59; Richardson, *Wacousta* (McClelland ᵈ Stewart); Mrs. Leprohon, *Antoinette de Mirecourt.* ᵉ also Baker, Chapter XI; Pierce, pp. 23–9; Logan, ᵃpter V; biography of Richardson by W. R. Riddell in ᵃkers of Canadian Literature (Ryerson).

CHAPTER 10: William Kirby;—Broadus, pp. 119–32; *ᵉ Golden Dog* (Musson). See also Pierce, pp. 27–9, *ᵈ William Kirby* (1929) (Macmillan); MacMechan, 135–6; biography of Kirby by W. R. Riddell in Makers *Canadian Literature (Ryerson).*

CHAPTER 11: Sir Gilbert Parker;—Broadus, pp. ᵒ–18, 132–48; *Seats of the Mighty* (Copp Clark Co.). also Pierce, pp. 29–32; MacMechan, pp. 139–42.

CHAPTER 12: Other Novelists, Historical and Region- —"Connor", preferably *Black Rock;* Marshall Saunders, *ᵉ à Charlitte* (also entitled *Rose of Acadie*); L. M. ᵑtgomery, the Emily books (McClelland and Stewart); ᵉith", *A Gentleman Adventurer* (the same); Stringer, *ᵘely O'Malley* (the same) or the prairie trilogy (the ᵉ). See also Pierce, pp. 32–9; Logan, Chapter XVI, *ᴵ (to p. 306), written by French.

CHAPTER 13: Some Recent Novelists;—Broadus, pp. ᵒ–9, 302–18; Stead, *Grain* or *The Smoking Flax* (both *Clelland and Stewart); de la Roche, *Possession* (Mac-

millan); Salverson, *The Viking Heart* (McClelland a
Stewart); Grove, *Our Daily Bread* (Macmillan).
also Pierce, pp. 39–44; Logan, pp. 306–13.

CHAPTER 14: Nature Writers I — Writers of Anir
Stories;—Saunders,*Beautiful Joe* (Baptist Book Roon
Roberts, *Kindred of the Wild* (Copp Clark Co.); Set
Wild Animals I Have Known or *Animal Heroes;* W.
Fraser, *Mooswa* (Briggs); McKishnie, *Openway* (M
son). See also Broadus, pp. 260–9; Pierce, pp. 151
Logan, pp. 250–4.

CHAPTER 15: Nature Writers II—Local Colourists
Broadus, pp. 269–301, 318–9; MacMechan, *The Book
Ultima Thule* (McClelland and Stewart); Grove, *O
Prairie Trails, The Turn of the Year* (Macmilla
"Hale", *Canadian Cities of Romance* (McClelland); Bl
In a Fishing Country, Brown Waters (both Macmilla
Heming, *The Drama of the Forest* (Doubleday, Doran,
Gundy); S. T. Wood, *Rambles of a Canadian Natura*
(Dutton). See also Pierce, pp. 100–1, 133–6; Log
Chapter XXXVII.

CHAPTER 16: Canadian Essayists;—Osler, *Aequan̄*
tas . . . or *An Alabama Student . . . ;* O'Hagan, *Canad
Essays* (Briggs), *Intimacies in Canadian Life and Let*
(Graphic); MacMechan, *The Life of a Little Col*
(Houghton Mifflin); Leacock, *Essays and Literary Stu*
(Doubleday, Doran, and Gundy); Deacon, *Po*

[272]

(Graphic). See also Pierce, pp. 129–36; Logan, Chapter XXVIII; Grove, *It Needs To be Said.*

CHAPTER 17: Canadian Humorists;—De Mille, *The Dodge Club;* Sara Jeanette Duncan, *A Social Departure;* Leacock, *Sunshine Sketches* . . . (Doubleday, Doran and Gundy); Peter McArthur, *Around Home* (Musson). *In Pastures Green* (Dent). See also Pierce, pp. 161–73.

CHAPTER 18: The Canadian Short Story;—Knister, *Canadian Short Stories* (Macmillan). See also Pierce, pp. 39, 43–4, 120, 167–8; Logan, Chapter XVII (by French).

CHAPTER 19: Canadian Drama;—Mair, *Tecumseh;* Campbell, *Poetical Tragedies;* Norwood, *Witch of Endor, Man of Kerioth* (McClelland and Stewart); Pickthall, *The Wood Carver's Wife* (same); Denison, *The Unheroic North* (the same); *One-act Plays* . . . (Canadian Authors' Association, Montreal Branch); *Plays From Hart House Theatre* (two volumes, Macmillan). See also Pierce, pp. 114–21; Logan, Chapter XXII, XXIV.

CHAPTER 20: Early Poets;—Broadus, pp. 7–16, 20–4, 33–40, 49–53, 342–8; Garvin, pp. 3–36, 97–104. See also Baker, Chapters XIV–XVIII; Pierce, pp. 62–70; Logan, Chapter V.

CHAPTER 21: Charles G. D. Roberts;—Broadus, pp. 76–81; Garvin, pp. 37–48; *Complete Poems* (Copp Clark Co.). See also Pierce, pp. 71–3; MacMechan, pp. 117–26;

Logan, Chapter VI, VII; Cappon, *Roberts and his Time* (Briggs) and *Charles G. D. Roberts* (Makers of Canadian Literature, Ryerson).

CHAPTER 22: Bliss Carman;—Broadus, pp. 70–6; Garvin, pp. 85-96; *Later Poems* and *Ballads and Lyrics* (McClelland and Stewart). See also Pierce, pp. 73-6; Mac-Mechan, pp. 126-33; Logan, Chapter IX; Odell Shepard, *Bliss Carman* (McClelland and Stewart).

CHAPTER 23: William Wilfred Campbell;—Broadus, pp. 81–5; Garvin, pp. 73–84; *Poetical Works* (Hodder and Stoughton). See also Pierce, pp. 76–8; MacMechan, pp. 133–5; Logan, Chapter XI.

CHAPTER 24: E. Pauline Johnson;—Broadus, pp. 88–92; Garvin, pp. 125-34; *Legends of Vancouver* (McClelland and Stewart). See also Pierce, pp. 78–81; Logan, Chapter XII.

CHAPTER 25: Archibald Lampman;—Broadus, pp. 60–9; Garvin, pp. 49–60; *Lyrics of Earth, Sonnets and Ballads* (Musson). See also Pierce, pp. 81–4; MacMechan, pp. 109–17; Logan, Chapter VIII; Guthrie, *The Poetry of Archibald Lampman;* Connor, *Archibald Lampman,* (Carrier).

CHAPTER 26: Frederick George Scott;—Broadus, pp. 59–60; Garvin, pp. 61–72; *Poems, Old and New* (Briggs). See also Pierce, pp. 86–7; Logan, Chapter XIII.

[274]

CHAPTER 27: Duncan Campbell Scott;—Garvin, pp. 105–16; *Poems of Duncan Campbell Scott* (McClelland and Stewart). See also *In the Village of Viger or The Witching of Elspie* (McClelland and Stewart); Pierce, pp. 84–6; Logan, Chapter X.

CHAPTER 28: Other Canadian Poets to Service;— Broadus, pp. 85–88; Garvin, pp. 117–24, 135–50, 163–206, 221–8, 235–62, 299–312, 345–50, 363–72, 449–54. See also Pierce, pp. 88–97; Logan, Chapter XIV.

CHAPTER 29: Canadian Poets since Service;—Broadus, 92–101; Garvin, pp. 207–20, 229–34, 263–98, 313–44, 351–62, 373–448, 455–530. See also Pierce, pp. 97–109; Logan, Chapter XIX, XX.

CHAPTER 30: William Henry Drummond;—Broadus, pp. 53–9; Garvin, pp. 151–62; *Complete Poems* (McClelland and Stewart). See also MacMechan, pp. 87–94; Logan, Chapter XVIII.

CHAPTER 31: French-Canadian Literature;—Broadus, pp. 238-60; Rivard, *Chez Nous* (in English, McClelland and Stewart); Hémon, *Maria Chapdelaine* (in English, Macmillan). See also MacMechan, Chapter II, IV; Pierce, II of Chapter I and I of subsequent chapters.

CHAPTER 32: Conclusion: See also Pierce, Chapter XIII.

INDEX

Acadia, ... 46

Acadian, the 42

Aikins, C., ... 155, 157

Albertan, ... 105

Alexander, W. J., ... 128

Alline, H., ... 20, 24, 63, 161

Alpatok, ... 114

American Boys' Series, ... 139

American Mercury, ... 133

Ame Solitaire, L', ... 258

Anciens Canadiens, Les, ... 256

Animal Stories, ... 111-118

Anne Books, ... 101

Anne of Avonlea, ... 101

Anne of Green Gables, ... 101

Anne of the Island, ... 101

Antoine, A., ... 155

"Apostle of Nova Scotia", ... 22

Archibald Lampman, ... 201-207

Arnold, M., ... 187, 202

Atlantic Monthly, ... 105, 179, 186

Attaché, The, ... 52, 53
Audobon, ... 109
Autobiography of a Fisherman, ... 103

Bailey, Jacob, ... 27, 29, 31
Baker, Ray Palmer, ... 23, 41, 128
Ballads and Lyrics, ... 183
Ballads and Sea-Songs of Nova Scotia, ... 35
Barham, ... 48
Baudelaire, ... 172
Beautiful Joe, ... 114
Beautiful Joe's Paradise, ... 114
Beautiful Rebel, A, ... 187
Behind the Arras, ... 181, 182
Behind the Veil, ... 139
Belt, T., ... 109
Ben Hur, ... 139
Benson, Mary Josephine, ... 244
Bibaud, M., ... 252
Bill Boram, ... 96, 237
Birds of Manitoba, ... 117
Black Rock, ... 99
Blake, W. H., ... 124-125
Blewett, Jean, ... 117, 227
Blue Castle, The, ... 101, 102
Blue Homespun, ... 241
Blue Water, ... 103
Bonny Prince Fetlar, ... 114

Book of the High Romance, The, ...   69

Book of the Native, The, ...   172

Book of Ultima Thule, The, ...   132

Boston Transcript, ...   149

Bowman, Louise Morey, ...   261

B. O. W. C. Series, ...   139

Brave Hearts, ...   116

Brown Waters, ...   125

Browne, Sir T., ...   129

Browning, R., ...   121, 187

Bulletin (Auburn), ...   149

Burns, R., ...   36, 38

Burroughs, J., ...   109

Byron, ...   72, 82

Call, F. O., ...   244

Cameron, G. F., ...   161, 168-169

Campbell, T., ...   185

Campbell, W. W., ... 154, 185-192, 202, 209, 212, 261

Canada, ...   187

Canadian Ballads, ...   164

Canadian Brothers, The, ...   76

Canadian Century, ...   151

Canadian Crusoes, ...   62

Canadian Essays, ...   131

Canadian Fisherman, ...   151

Canadian Idylls, ...   80

Canadian Plays from Hart House Theatre, ...   157

Canadien Errant, Un, ... 255
"Canuck, Janey" (Mrs. Emily Murphy), ... 129, 132-133
Cappon, J., ... 128
Captain Salvation, ... 103
Carman, Bliss, ... 128, 170, 178-184, 217, 226, 261
Cartier, Sir Etienne, ... 89
Casgrain, Abbé H. R., ... 255
Chap Book, ... 179
Chez Nous, ... 125, 251
Christian Science Monitor, ... 133
Churchill, C., ... 30
Chute, A. H., ... 103-104
Clockmaker, The, ... 52, 53
Club, The, ... 45, 47, 50
Coleman, Helena 226
Coleridge, S. T., ... 187
Connor, C. Y., ... 201
"Connor, Ralph" (Rev. C. W. Gordon), .. 95, 96, 99, 100
Cotes, Mrs. Everard (See Duncan, Sara Jeanette)
Courier (Amherstburg), ... 164
Courier (Crystal City), ... 104
Crawford, Isabella Valancy, ... 161, 166-168, 235
Crémazie, O., ... 252, 253, 254
"Crichton, John" (N. G. Guthrie), ... 201
Current Literature, ... 179

Daily News (Kingston), ... 164
Daily News (Toronto), ... 233

Dalton, Annie Charlotte, ...   227
Darwin, C., ...   109
Daulac, ...   154
Day, F P., ... 96, 104
Deacon, W. A., ... 129, 133-134
Delight, ... 106
De Mille, Jas., ... 137-139
Denison, M., ... 155, 157, 262
De Quincey, T., ...   13
Deserted Village, The, ...   82
Dickens, C., ... 54, 150
Dickinson, J., ...   30
Dodge Club, The, ...   139
Dominion Illustrated, ...   125
Drama, ... 152-159
Drama of the Forest, ...   125
Drummond, W. H., ... 137, 148, 161, 243-250
Dryden, J.   30
Duncan, Norman, ... 146, 149-150
Duncan, Sara Jeanette (Mrs. Everard Cotes), 137, 140-141

Eaton, A. W. H., ...   226
Ecarté, ...   75
Echo des Jeunes, ...   256
Edgar, P., ...   128
Elton Hazelwood, ...   209
Emerson, R. W., ... 170, 189, 229
Emigrant, The, ...   37

Emily Books, ... 101, 102

Emily's Quest, ... 100

Essay, The, ... 127-134, 262-263

Evangeline, ... 196, 254

Evening Post (New York), ... 133, 149

Explorers of the Dawn, ... 106

Far Horizons, ... 183

"Farewell, A.," 29

Faust, ... 90

Fielding, H., ... 185

Fishing Gazette, ... 151

Four Jameses, The, ... 134

Fraser, W. A., ... 113, 115-116, 146

Fréchette, L., ... 254-255, 257

Free Theatre, ... 155

Friendship of Art, The, ... 179

Garneau, F. X., ... 252

Garvin, Mrs. Amelia Beers ("Katherine Hale"), 124, 233-4

Garvin, J. W., ... 233

Gaspé, P. A. de, ... 256

Gazette (Halifax), ... 42

Gazette (Montreal), ... 165

Gems of Poetry, ... 197

General Description of Nova Scotia, A, ... 49

Gentleman Adventurer, A., ... 98

Gérin-Lajoie, ... 255

Globe (Toronto), ... 124, 141, 147, 165, 186

Glooscap, ... 194-195, 196

God of Gods, The 155

Golden Dickie, ... 114

Golden, Dog, The, ... 84, 86, 93, 94, 110

Goldsmith, O., (English), ... 44, 82, 161

Goldsmith, O., (Canadian), ... 161-162

Gomery, P., ... 104

Gordon, Rev. C. W. ("Ralph Connor"), ... 99-100

"Grafton, Garth" (Sara Jeanette Duncan), ... 141

Grain, ... 105

Great War as I Saw it, The, ... 209

Grove, F. P., ... 69, 104, 108-110, 124, 262

Guthrie, N. G. ("John Crichton"), ... 201

"Hale, Katherine" (Mrs. Garvin), ... 124, 233-234

Haliburton, T. C., ... 30, 47-54, 63

Harper's, ... 125, 149, 186

Harris, J. C., ... 112

Harrison, Mrs. S. F. ("Seranus"), ... 225, 244

Heavysege, C., ... 154

Heming, A. H. H., ... 124, 125-126

Hémon, L., ... 125, 251

Henry, Alexander, ... 55-56

Henry V, ... 90

Hiawatha, ... 195-196

Hidden Places. 103

Histoire du Canada, ... 252

Historical and Statistical Account of Nova Scotia, ... 49

History of Canada, ... 67-69

Holland, Norah Mary (Mrs. J. D. Claxton), ... 232-233

Holmes, O. W., ... 236

Hood, R. A., ... 104

Howe, John, ... 42, 44

Howe, Joseph, ... 40-46,-49, 63, 161, 163

Howells, W. D., ... 196, 255

Huckleberry Finn, ... 98

Humorists, ... 135-143

Hutton, M., ... 128

Hymns, ... 24-25

Ian of the Orcades, ... 187

Idylls of the King, ... 83

Illustrated American, ... 171

In a Fishing Country, ... 125

Independent, ... 179

Ingersoll, W. E., ... 145

Innocents Abroad, ... 139

In Old France and New, ... 243

In Pastures Green, ... 142

In the Garden of Charity, ... 96

In the Village of Viger, ... 218, 243

Intimacies in Canadian Life and Letters, ... 131

Iron Door, The, ... 241

It Needs to be Said, ... 109

Jacob, F., ... 158

Jalna, ... 106-107

Jameson, Mrs. Anna, ... 12, 59,123-124, 263

Jimmy Gold-Coast, ... 114

Johnson, Emily Pauline, ... 18, 193-200, 235, 261

Journal (Bailey's), ... 27, 31

Judgment House, The, ... 92

Keats, J., ... 166, 171, 202, 226

"Keith, Marian" (Mrs. Mary Esther (Miller)
     MacGregor), ... 95, 98

Khayyam, Omar, ... 229

Kidnapped, ... 148

Kilmeny of the Orchard, ... 101

King, W. B. ("Basil"), ... 95, 96

Kirby, W., ... 79-86, 93

Kinister, R., ... 145

Lake Lyrics, ... 186, 209

Lampman, A.,
     ...... 121, 186, 189, 201-207, 218, 219, 259, 261, 264

Land of Singing Waters, ... 240

Lanigan, G. T., ... 137, 139-140

Later Poems, ... 183

Laurier, Sir W., ... 89

Leacock, S. B., ... 137, 142-143

Legende d'un Peuple, ... 255

Legends of the Micmacs, ... 194, 199

Legends of Vancouver, ...   198

Le May, P., ...   254

Leprohon, Mrs. Rosanna, ...   77

Lever, C., ...   148

Life and Journals (Alline's), ...   20-24

Lighthall, W. D., ...   95, 225

Literary Garland, ...   72, 76, 77, 164

Little Admiral, The, ...   16, 243

Little Theatre Movement, ...   155-159

Living Forest, The   125

Local Colourists, ...   119-126

Logan, J. D., ...   128, 226

Lonely O'Malley, ...   98

Longfellow, H. W., ...   172, 195-196, 254

Lord of the Silver Dragon, ...   108

Loyalist Literature, ...   26-32

Lozeau, A., ...   258-259, 264

Lyrics of the Earth, Sonnets and Ballads, ...   201

McArthur, P., ...   124, 137, 141-142

Macaulay, T. B., ...   65-66

McClung, Mrs. Nellie, ...   95

McClure's, ...   149

Macdonald, Sir J. A., ...   89, 186, 216

Macdonald, W., ...   237-239

McGee, T. D., ...   161, 163

Machar, Agnes Maule, ...   95

McIlwraith, Jean, ...   16, 148, 243

McInnes, T. R. E., ... 228-229

Mackay, Mrs. Isabel Ecclestone, ... 104, 227

Mackenzie, A., ... 57-58

MacKenzie, W. R., ... 35,

McKishnie, A. P., ... 113, 117-118

McLachlan, A., ... 36-39, 63, 161

McLennan, W., ... 146, 148, 243

MacMechan, ... 124, 128, 131-132

MacMurchy, A., ... 128

MacPhail, A., ... 128

Magic for Marigold, ... 101

Mail (Niagara), ... 81

Mail and Empire (Toronto), ... 133, 141, 233

Mair, C., ... 154, 161, 165-166

Making of Personality, The, ... 180

Mammals of Manitoba, ... 117

Man of Kerioth, The, ... 155

Man who Slept till Noon, The, ... 145

Maria Chapdelaine, ... 125, 251

Marquis, T. G., ... 95, 128

Marshall, W. E., ... 226

Marsh Hay, ... 155

Mates of the Tangle, ... 118

Matins, ... 227

Melville Island, ... 42

Mitchell, S. Weir, ... 245-246, 249

Montcalm, ... 255

Montgomery, L. M. (Mrs. Ewan Macdonald), 95, 100-102

Moodie, Mrs. Susanna, ... 60-61, 124, 263

Moore, T., ... 228, 229

Mooswa, ... 115-116

Morin, P., ... 259-260

Movements of the British Legion, ... 74

Much Ado about Nothing, ... 137

Murphy, Mrs. Emily ("Janey Canuck"), ... 132-133

My Lattice and Other Poems, ... 210

My Pets, ... 114

My Spanish Sailor, ... 114

National Consciousness, ... 265-267

Nature and Human Nature, ... 53

Nature Writers, ...111-126

Neighbours, ... 105

Nelligan, E., ... 257-258

Newfoundland Verse, ... 240

"New Lights", ... 20

News (Kingston), ... 168

News-Letter, ... 42

Nita, ... 114

Norwood, R. W., ... 155, 236-237

Nova Scotia, ... 38

Nova Scotia Magazine, ... 31-32

Novascotian, ... 43, 45

Novel, ... 71-110

Odell, J., ... 29-31, 161

O'Hagan, T., ...   129, 130-131

Old Province Tales, ...   132

One-Act Plays, ...   155-159

Openway, ...   118

Osborne, Marian, ...   158, 261

Osler, Sir W., ...   129-130

Our Daily Bread, ...   110

Over Prairie Trails, ...   109

Oxford Book of American Verse, ...   179

Oxford Book of Canadian Verse, ...   179

Papineau, ...   255

Parker, Sir G., ...   85-86, 87-94, 146

Parkin, Sir G. R., ...   89, 171, 178

Parnassiens, ...   256, 259

Pèlerinage au Pays d'Evangeline, ...   255

Pens and Pirates, ...   134

Pickwick Papers, ...   150

Pickthall, Marjorie, L. C., ...   158, 234-235

Pickthall, Marmaduke, ...   234

Pierce, L., ...   128, 194

Pierre, ...   243

Pierre and his People, ...   91

Pine, Rose and Fleur-de-Lis, ...   244

Poe, E A., ...   228, 253, 258

Poems and Essays, ...   46

Poetical Tragedies, ...   154

Poetry of Archibald Lampman, ...   202

Poetry of Life, The, ... 179-180

Poor Man's Rock, ... 103

Pope, A., ... 30, 82

Possession, ... 106, 108

Poteen, ... 134

Prairie Child, The, ... 97

Prairie Mother, The, ... 97

Prairie Wife, The, ... 97

Pratt, E. J. 240-241

Puritan Literature, ... 18-25

Pussy Black-Face, ... 114

Quebec Magazine, ... 32

Queen's Birthday, The, ... 83

Quo Vadis, ... 139

Rambles of a Canadian Naturalist, ... 124

Rand, S. T., ... 194

Rand, T. H., ... 225

Reade, C., ... 138

Red Cow and her Friends, The, ... 142

Review (Cartwright), ... 104

Religio Medici, ... 129

Rhymes of a Rounder, ... 229

Richardson, Major J., ... 72-77, 84, 85

Right of Way, The, ... 93

Rising Village, The, ... 161

Rivard, A., ... 125, 251

River of Strangers, ... 104

Roberts, C. G. D., ... 67-68, 95, 113, 115, 121, 146,
    170-177, 178, 180, 189, 217, 219, 226, 259, 261, 264

Roberts, L., ... 261

Roberts, T. G., ... 95

Roche, Mazo de la, ... 104, 105-107, 158

Rockbound, ... 96, 103

Rogers, Mrs. Grace McLeod, ... 146, 148-149

Roosevelt and the Antinoe, The, ... 241

Rosary of Pan, The, ... 240

Rose à Charlitte (Rose of Acadie), ... 114

Rossetti, D. G., ... 172

Roughing It in the Bush, ... 61

Runner, The, ... 99

Sagas of the Sea, ... 132

Salverson, Laura Goodman, ... 104, 107-107

Sam Slick's Wise Saws and Modern Instances, ... 53

Sanctuary, ... 183

Sangster, C., ... 161, 164-5

Sappho, ... 168

Saturday Night, ... 133

Saturday Review of Literature, ... 133

Saul, ... 154

Saunders, M. Marshall, ... 95, 113-115

Sa'-Zada Tales, ... 116

Scott, D. C.,
    146, 148, 158, 186, 201, 216-223, 243, 259, 261, 264

Scott, F. G., ... 208-215, 261

Scott, Sir W., ...   47, 72, 74, 82

Scottish Literature, ...   33-39

Search for America, A, ...   69, 109

Seats of the Mighty, ...   93-94

"Seranus" (Mrs. S. Frances Harrison), ...   225-244

Service, R. W., ...   229-231, 235

Seton, E. T., ...   112, 113, 115

Settlers of the Marsh, ...   110

Shack Locker, ...   151

Shakespeare, ...   153-154, 155, 191

Shelley, P. B., ...   168

Sherman, F., ...   226

Shining Ship, The, ...   227

Short Stories, ...   144-151

Simcoe, J. C., ...   218

Sinclair, B. W., ...   103

Sky Pilot, The, ...   99

Slick Series, ...   49-54, 139

Smoking Flax, The, ...   105

Smythe, A. E. S., ...   226

Snowflakes and Sunbeams, ...   186

Social Departure, A, ...   141

Soirées Canadiennes, ...   253

Soirées du Chateau de Ramezay, ...   257

Songs from Vagabondia, ...   180

Songs of the Common Day, ...   172

Soul's Quest and Other Poems, The, ...   210

Spanish John, ...   148

Span of Life, The, ... 148

Spirit Lake, ... 125

Spirit of Canadian Literature, ... 263

Standard (Montreal), ... 132

Stansbury, J., ... 28-29, 161

Star (Montreal), ... 140

Star (Toronto), ... 230

Stead, R. J. C., ... 104-105

Stephen, A. M., ... 239-240

Stephen, Sir L., ... 239

Stevenson, R. L., ... 148

Stories of the Land of Evangeline, ... 149

Strickland, Agnes, ... 60

Strickland, Samuel, ... 60

Stringer, A., ... 95, 97-98, 146

Sue, E., ... 138

Sunday World, ... 118

Swinburne, A. C., ... 172

Syllabus of Canadian Literature, ... 268-275

Talks on Poetry and Life, ... 180

Tecumseh (Mair's), ... 154

Tecumseh (Richardson's), ... 72, 75

Tekahionwake (E. Pauline Johnson), ... 193

Tennyson, A., ... 77, 83, 187, 210

Testament of the Ancient One, ... 228

Thackeray, W. M., ... 148

Thomson, E. W., ... 137, 147

Thoreau, H. D., ...   109
Thoroughbreds, ...   116
Times (London), ...   74
Times (New York), ...   133
Titans, The, ...   240
Tom Sawyer, ...   98
Traill, Mrs. Catharine Parr, ...   61-62, 113, 124
Travels and Adventures, ...   56
Treading the Winepress, ...   96
Trotter, B. F., ...   241-242
Truth, ...   142
Turn of the Year, The, ...   109
"Twain, Mark", ...   54, 139

U. E. A Tale of Uppper Canada, ...   81
Uncle Tom's Cabin, ...   15
Unnamed Lake and Other Poems, The, ...   211

Virgil, ...   82
Verne, J., ...   138
Viking Blood, The, ...   103, 151
Viking Heart, The, ...   108
Villon, F., ...   229
Voyages from Montreal, ...   58

Wacousta, ...   75, 76
Wallace, F. W., ...   103, 146, 150-151
Wandering Dog, The, ...   114
"Ward, Artemus", ...   54

Watson, A. D., ...   226
Watson, R., ...   103
Weavers, The, ...   92
Week, ...   171, 197
Weekly Chronicle, ...   42
Western Tribune, ...   239
Wetherald, A. Ethelwyn, ...   225
When Sparrows Fall, ...   108
When Valmond Came to Pontiac, ...   93
Whig (Kingston), ...   164
Whitefield, ...   20
Whiteoaks of Jalna, The, ...   106
Whitman, W., ...   229
Wild Garden, ...   183
Williams, M., ...   69
Winter Studies and Summer Rambles in Canada, ...   59
Witch of Endor, The, ...   155
Witches' Brew, The, ...   240
Witching of Elspie, The, ...   218
Wood, S. T., ...   124
Wood, Lieut.-Col. W. C. H., ...   70
Wood Carver's Wife, The, ...   158
Wood Myth and Fable, ...   112
Wordsworth, W., ...   121, 172, 187, 206, 207
World (New York), ...   140

Young Dodge Club Series, ...   139
Youth's Companion, ...   147